SPEECH PLAY AND

T0097902

The publication of this book was assisted by a University Cooperative Society Subvention Grant awarded by the University of Texas at Austin.

Speech Play and Verbal Art

BY JOEL SHERZER

UNIVERSITY OF TEXAS PRESS, AUSTIN

COPYRIGHT © 2002 BY THE UNIVERSITY OF TEXAS PRESS

All rights reserved

Printed in the United States of America

First edition, 2002

Requests for permission to reproduce material from this work
should be sent to Permissions, University of Texas Press,
P.O. Box 7819, Austin, TX 78713-7819.

⊗ The paper used in this book meets the minimum requirements
of ANSI/NISO Z39.48-1992 (R1997) (Permanence of Paper).

LIBRARY OF CONGRESS CATALOGING-IN-PUBLICATION DATA

Sherzer, Joel.
  Speech play and verbal art / by Joel Sherzer.
     p.   cm.
Includes bibliographical references and index.
  ISBN 0-292-77768-x (hardcover : alk. paper) —
ISBN 0-292-77769-8 (pbk. : alk. paper)
  1. Play on words.   2. Word games.   3. Figures of speech.
4. Joking.   5. Riddles.   I. Title.
P304 .S53   2002
401'.41—dc21

                              2001008474

Contents

Preface

One morning during April of 1970 I was in Panama, traveling in a canoe to the Kuna island of Mulatuppu with some Kuna friends. We were coming from the mainland forest, where I had helped them plant crops. This was not long after my arrival in what was then called San Blas, now Kuna Yala, and I was very much in my first struggling stages of trying to speak and understand the Kuna language. I was good enough at it to be able to communicate in a very rudimentary way and was already the butt of jokes for my (lack of) linguistic ability. On that particular morning, all of a sudden, I could not understand anything the others were saying, not a single word. I first attributed this to fatigue as well as to the possibility that I had by chance come upon a conversation involving vocabulary totally new to me. In any case the others were speaking to me and I was totally lost. Then I suddenly realized that a joke was involved and the joke was on me. The Kuna were speaking *sorsik sunmakke* 'talking backwards,' in which the syllables of words are reversed. This simple bit of linguistic play was enough to make the Kuna language, already hard enough for me, totally incomprehensible, and to cause the Kuna individuals with me to laugh riotously at my double difficulties with the Kuna language—backwards as well as frontwards. As it turns out, at that time I had been working on an analysis of Kuna sound patterns, in particular the best way to deal with the abstract representation of Kuna consonants. This play language, as I have now come to call it, precisely by moving syllables around within words proved to be extremely useful for my analysis and my understanding of Kuna individuals' own mental representation of their language. From that moment on, in addition to and indeed because of being the butt of endless jokes, I began to realize the importance of speech play in Kuna language, culture, and society. The study of speech play has figured more and more prominently in my research dealing with the Kuna and has rewarded me with insight into the nature of Kuna thought and action. Because of that first experience with speech play and the rewards it led to for me, I have explored play languages and other forms of play not only among the Kuna but in other places in the world, in particular in Latin America, in Brazil, Colombia, Mexico, and Panama; in Europe, in France and Italy; and in Asia, in Bali, Indonesia. This book is the outcome of these explorations.

In addition to that initial experience among the Kuna and many subsequent ones, among the Kuna and elsewhere, a number of events, occasions, and people have contributed to my understanding of speech play. In 1971, along with Barbara Kirshenblatt-Gimblett, I organized a session dealing with speech play at the annual meeting of the Anthropological Association of America. That session led to the publication of a book called *Speech Play*, edited by Barbara Kirshenblatt-Gimblett, with an introduction we jointly wrote. During the years I have been at the University of Texas at Austin, I have from time to time jointly taught courses dealing with speech play and verbal art, namely with my colleagues Steven Feld, Dina Sherzer, and Anthony Woodbury. I have learned greatly from these experiences.

There are many other scholars who have contributed to my understanding of speech play and verbal art. I would like to indicate four. Dell Hymes, my mentor in the approach to language and culture known as the ethnography of speaking, introduced me to the notion of speech play and verbal art as cultural foci. His work in these areas is a constant inspiration. Richard Bauman, my colleague for many years at the University of Texas, was my closest collaborator there in developing a program in linguistic anthropology, with the study of speech play and verbal art of central concern—as it was in the book we edited together, *Explorations in the Ethnography of Speaking*. Erving Goffman, through publications and conversations, provided me and continues to provide me with insights into the nature of social interaction. His concept of frame is crucial to this book. Américo Paredes's scholarly work serves as a constant reminder of the importance of humor and play for an understanding of culture and the crucial necessity of paying serious attention to speech play and verbal art during field research. I am fortunate to have had this wonderful man as a colleague and friend. Antonio Pasqualino, a close friend and collaborator, was a brilliant man who, in addition to being a well-known surgeon, dedicated his life to the maintenance and study of Sicilian popular culture, in particular puppetry. His warmth and collegiality, along with his important scholarship, are very important to me.

In addition to the speakers and performers acknowledged throughout the book, my understanding of Balinese speech play and verbal art was enhanced by discussions with I. Wayan Kerja and I. Made Dharmayasa, and my understanding of Kuna speech play and verbal art was augmented by discussions with Hortenciano Martínez and Anselmo Urrutia.

Portions and versions of what I have written here were previously presented at conferences, congresses, and seminars. These include meetings of the American Anthropological Association and the International Society for the Study of Humor; a 1990 conference at Texas A&M University on repetition in discourse; a 1992 conference at Portland State University in honor of Dell Hymes, entitled "Ways of Speaking/Ways of Knowing"; a 1997 conference at the University of Costa Rica on linguistics and literature; and lectures at the following universities: Michigan, Panama, Texas, Virginia, and Zurich. In addition, an earlier version of the book benefited from the comments of Ellen Basso and Dina Sherzer.

My research dealing with speech play and verbal art in various places would not have been possible without financial support from several sources over the years. These sources include fellowships from the John Simon Guggenheim Foundation and the National Endowment for the Humanities as well as grants from the National Science Foundation, the National Institute of Mental Health, and the University of Texas, through the university's Research Institute and the Institute for Latin American Studies.

In order to write this book I have been closely attentive, with ears and eyes, and with tape recorder whenever possible, to the great variety of speech play and verbal art in the world around me. Once you see the world from the perspective that I adopt here, you never see it otherwise. This is a book I have very much enjoyed working on, for a combination of reasons ranging from the theoretical perspective it proposes to my sheer enjoyment of the many examples. It is also, because it has provided so much pleasure, a book which I secretly hoped never to finish.

SPEECH PLAY AND VERBAL ART

CHAPTER I

Introduction

Everything that we have so far seen to be true of language points to the fact that it is the most significant and colossal work that the human spirit has evolved—nothing short of a finished form of expression for all communicable experience. This form may be endlessly varied by the individual without thereby losing its distinctive contours; and it is constantly reshaping itself as is all art. Language is the most massive and inclusive art we know, a mountainous and anonymous work of unconscious generations.
—Edward Sapir, *Language*

This book is about speech play, and particularly the significance of speech play in the intersection of language, culture, and society and in relation to verbal art. It is intended to be exploratory, suggestive, provocative, and fun(ny). My argument is that play, especially speech play, which has been marginalized and trivialized in the disciplines of anthropology and linguistics, among others, should actually be central to these disciplines, both theoretically and methodologically. Speech play provides implicit and explicit metacommentary—in the form of both the praxis of everyday life and artistic performance—on systems and structure, social and cultural as well as interactional and (socio)linguistic. It explores and indeed flirts with the boundaries of the socially, culturally, and linguistically possible and appropriate; for this reason it is often felt to be simultaneously humorous, serious, and aesthetically pleasing. Speech play can be deeply serious and significant. It is precisely because it is so important that it is so widespread in the world.

Definitions and Issues

Speech play is the manipulation of elements and components of language in relation to one another, in relation to the social and cultural contexts of language use, and against the backdrop of other verbal possibilities in which it is not foregrounded. The elements manipulated can be at any level of language, from sound patterns to syntax, semantics, and discourse; they can include the various languages used in multilingual situations, and can involve nonverbal communication. Speech play can be conscious or unconscious, noticed or not noticed, purposeful or nonpurposeful, and humorous or serious. Nonetheless, given the focus on manipulation, speech play typically involves a degree of selection and consciousness beyond that of ordinary language use.

The various meanings of the word *play*, in English as well as other languages, are all relevant to this book. One meaning is manipulation and along with it freedom, but always within a set of rules. We talk of the play of a door or window within their frames, the little give-and-take that they have so they are not completely tight. In language the different ways of pronouncing the same word or expressing the same or related ideas are quite analogous to this sense of play. No doubt Edward Sapir had this sense of play in mind when he used the term "consonantal play" in describing a fascinating case of sound symbolism in the Nootka language of Vancouver Island: "Consonantal play consists either in altering certain consonants of a word, in this case sibilants, to other consonants that are phonetically related to them, or in inserting meaningless consonants or consonant clusters in the body of the word. The physical classes indicated by these methods are children, unusually fat or heavy people, unusually short adults, those suffering from some defect of the eye, hunchbacks, those that are lame, left-handed persons, and circumcised males."[1] *Play* is also an appropriate word to describe the lack of perfect fit between and among the various levels, components, and modules of language, what Sapir expressed in the provocative phrase "All grammars leak."[2] This kind of play within language structure enables many of the verbal forms and processes I discuss. Another meaning of play is that of performance, as in the playing of a musical instrument. The concept of performance is crucial to my approach. Still another meaning of play is that of playing a game, which raises the interesting question of the relation between play and games. Not all play takes the form of games, with sides and winners and losers, but some forms, such as verbal dueling, quite clearly do. Finally there is the idea of play as the opposite of serious or literal, for which the Latin-derived term *ludic* has been used.

The word and the concept of play have a truly remarkable set of intersecting meanings and uses. *Webster's Third New International Dictionary of the English Language* has two pages of definitions for *play*.[3] Just some of these definitions, for *play* as a noun, are:

1. act of briskly handling, using, or plying a sword or other weapon or instrument: "gun play."
2. particular act, maneuver, or point in a game.
3. recreational activity.
4. jest, fun: "said or done in play."

5. deal, venture: "land play."
6. brisk, lively, or light activity involving change, variation, transition, or alternation: "the play of light and shadow on the dancing waves."
7. free of unimpeded motion (as part of a machine): "the cylinder has about an inch of play."
8. a move or series of moves calculated to arouse affection: "make a play for him."
9. alive: "in play."

And for *play* as a verb:

1. to toy or move aimlessly to and fro: "his hand was playing on the edge of the bed."
2. to deal or behave frivolously or mockingly.
3. to deal in a light or speculative manner: "to play the stock market."
4. to have an effect: "played upon my emotions."
5. pretend: "he played at being a doctor."
6. to put on a performance.
7. to put into action or motion.

Other languages and cultures combine these definitions and meanings of *play* in different ways.[4] French *jouer* like English *play* is used for manipulation, musical performance, games, and nonserious behavior such as joking and jesting. The Spanish cognate word *jugar* is used for manipulation and games as well as nonseriousness, while *tocar* (literally 'touch') is used for musical performance. In Kuna, *totoe* is used for playing and joking in the sense of tricking and fooling as well as playing games and dancing. The Indonesian word *main* signifies playing games as well as nonseriousness. In English and French, the word *play* is used for theatrical performance. In these languages and in fact in the Romance and Germanic languages more generally, as well as in Indonesian languages, it is also used with sexual denotations and connotations. In Kuna the word *pinsa*, placed before verbs, has the meaning 'for the fun of' or 'just for play,' as in *pinsa yartakke* 'tricking someone for the fun of it.' A similar function is achieved in Indonesian languages by means of reduplication, which is used to indicate that an object or activity is nonserious or for play. Thus Indonesian *mobil* 'car,' and *mobilmobilan* 'toy car.'

These different meanings of play lead us to the very useful notions of frame and metacommunication, as developed by such scholars as Gregory Bateson and Erving Goffman.[5] Frame is the definition, conception, or organization of an activity as either real or literal, rehearsed, practiced, talked about, lied about, dreamt, or fantasized. Play then is a type of frame. Related to frame is the concept of function of language and of communication more generally. In addition to functioning referentially, naming things and providing information about them, language functions socially, expressively, metacommunicatively, and poetically.[6] Speech play combines several of these functions. In turn, speech play, as a form of language use, has various functions, psychological, cultural, humorous, and artistic or poetic.

These functions of language in general and speech play in particular overlap with one another and can be minimized or foregrounded in particular instances. At one level no language use occurs without speech play and verbal art being involved to some degree. At the same time there are verbal forms in which speech play and/or verbal art are the central and total foci. The notion of consciousness and purpose is interesting here. Some forms of play are unconscious and unintended—certain sound or word associations, for example. Others are conscious, intended, and performed, such as jokes or stories. And there are various possibilities in between, as when an unintended pun draws laughter and becomes the focus of commentary. This provides us with an insight into the nature of humor, clearly related intimately to play. Many scholars, including Freud and Bergson, have noticed that humor results from surprise juxtapositions. The sudden coming into consciousness and public awareness of an unintended verbal play, along with the subsequent commentary, is a good example. Add to this the backdrop of entangled cultural and personal presuppositions and assumptions and we can begin to understand particular instances of humor, which can be quite complex.

Speech play is inherent in the formal structure of language. The intrinsic play aspects of language are exploited in rhetorical and poetic forms as well as in discourse more generally. They are also located in everyday speech, in the form of word associations, repetitions and parallelisms, and clever responses and comebacks which feel creatively poetic. Play is located, again both actually and potentially, in sociolinguistic situations, in the juxtaposition of languages, dialects, and styles in use. Yet while speech play is present to some degree in all speech—whether informal, formal, conversational, or artistic—it is most evident and focused in certain conventional forms of play found in many societies. These include play languages, puns, jokes, verbal dueling, proverbs, and riddles.

There is a close connection between speech play and verbal art. Speech play provides the means and resources, such as metaphor, parallelism, and narrative manipulations, out of which verbal art is created. At the same time, it serves various and overlapping ends: comic or humorous, religious, rhetorical, mnemonic, competitive, imitative, experimental, and artistic. Play, especially the juxtaposition of languages and verbal forms in various ways, is thus a major source of aesthetic creativity and innovation, in both oral and literate traditions.

Crucial to the theoretical perspective I advocate in this book is the existence of a loose fit, a loose coupling,[7] between and among the various components of language—phonology, morphology, syntax, semantics, and discourse—and between language and the various contexts and contextualizations of its use, both sociocultural and social interactional. This loose coupling generates literally endless forms of speech play and verbal art.

Settings

In this book I draw on my own research and observations of speech play and verbal art in various places: the United States; western Europe, especially France and Italy; Latin America, especially among the Kuna Indians of Panama and Panama more generally, as well as Mexico, Brazil, and the Caribbean; and Bali, Indonesia.

There is a significance to the ethnographic juxtaposition of these places. The United States is a paradigm, perhaps *the* paradigm, of a modern, complex, urban, multiethnic society. It is currently undergoing remarkable changes as the result of population movements and contacts and technological innovations. Social and cultural reality in the United States is both expressed and defined through traditional forms of speech play such as puns, jokes, and humorous stories; the fleeting speech play embedded in everyday interaction; and newly emerging forms such as the switching and mixing of languages and dialects and the invention of playful answering-machine messages and email communications.

As in all societies, in the United States speech play can be contrasted with referential, transactional speech. And again, as in all societies, in the United States speech play has its own special and particular ways of relating to referential and transactional speech. Speech play occurs among friends, and its informality is a marker of the social relationship we call friendship. It also occurs in interactions among individuals who are not necessarily friends but who participate together in various sorts of events. Thus speech play can be an *icebreaker*, as it is called in American English, at such events as casual meetings and parties. The metaphor here is revealing. Referential and transactional speech is cold, even icy or frigid, whereas speech play is warm. Notice also that such speech play occurs within "small talk"—another revealing metaphor, presumably to be contrasted with "big talk," which is serious. Speech play is time out and time off from the otherwise seriousness of the referential and transactional flow of life.

No study of speech play in the United States would be complete without paying attention to its remarkable social, cultural, and linguistic diversity, including, among others, the speech play of Native Americans, African Americans, Latinos, Asian Americans, and Jewish Americans, as well as various crisscrossing and intersecting diasporas.

As in the United States, speech play in France contrasts with referential and transactional speech. France has a long yet continually evolving tradition of slang, called *argot*, which is extremely playful and creative. While French politeness can be remarkably formal and personal space carefully protected from verbal intrusion, at the same time French conviviality enables the exchange of small talk and verbal play, even in such unlikely settings (at least to American observers) as between tables in restaurants. Nonetheless, in France, as elsewhere, the more informal the setting the more likely speech play will occur. The setting par excellence for French speech play continues to be the public, outdoor market, a setting going back to the Middle Ages that is still very much alive today.

In Latin America, speech play and verbal art have evolved from mixtures and blendings of indigenous, European (especially Iberian), and African traditions, and involve intersections of musical and verbal practice. They are manifested in everyday interaction and especially in the vibrant festivals characteristic of these places. In Brazil, both the ethic of the importance of extremely friendly, lighthearted interactions and their actual practice exist against the backdrop of brutal class differences and conflicts.[8] In Brazil as well as elsewhere in Latin America, traditional, indeed centuries-old forms of speech play such as the public telling of medieval epics coexist with the most contemporary of forms, providing a laboratory for the study of the relationship between orality and literacy.[9] There are many rituals and festivals throughout Latin America, in indigenous, European-origin, and Indian and African diasporic communities. These include indigenous curing and puberty rites, Mardi Gras celebrations and carnivals, and town and village patron-saint fiestas. These rituals and festivals constitute a rich, complex tradition and form the center of community and regional life—from social, cultural, historical, economic, ethnic, and religious points of view.

The Panamanian Kuna are a tropical-forest and island community who have managed to maintain their rich indigenous traditions in the context of living along the border of the encroaching, technological Western world. Among the Kuna, play and joking turn up everywhere, side by side and within the most serious forms of speech and action, and especially in conjunction with verbal art.[10] Speech play and verbal art clearly constitute cultural foci for the Kuna. They are continually and consciously aware of the aesthetic properties of language, most strikingly in ritual speech but in everyday speech as well. While Kuna speaking practices can be approached in terms of the sociocultural functions of speech, social control, political maneuvering, curing, magic, and puberty rituals, these functions are inextricably tied to the aesthetic function, to the pleasing playful and artistic properties of language. Indeed, it is by means of verbally artistic language that these other functions are achieved. In addition, the aesthetic and play functions of language are semi-independent of the referential or purely informational and transactional functions, working in the service of the latter while maintaining a potential for freedom of expression.

Bali is one of the most studied places in the world, the subject of research by anthropologists; art, drama, and music critics and performers; amateur and professional dancers and puppeteers; and tourists. It is a classically traditional and complex Asian society struggling to maintain its fascinating identity in the face of incredibly drastic change. Since anthropology has not entered play into its list of favored topics, even in societies such as Bali where it is clearly a cultural focus, very little has been written on the subject.[11] And yet in Balinese society—so well known for its grace, decorum, poise, etiquette, elegance, and refinement—wit, banter, and boisterous humor are omnipresent and cut across the boundaries of the everyday and the ceremonial and ritual, in part as a way of negotiating and constructing a unique identity within the Indonesian nation and the modern world. Much of Balinese speech play focuses on multilingualism and alternative speech levels and styles.

By examining speech play in these various places, I am able to provide a cross-cultural, comparative perspective which I believe is essential to the study of speech play and verbal art.

History and Relevance

The history of the study of speech play relates to several disciplines, including anthropology, linguistics, sociology, psychology, philosophy, literary criticism, and folklore.[12] Anthropologists have treated play and humor as either marginal or secondary to concerns traditionally considered more basic, such as social organization and kinship, or, more recently, political economy, ideology, ethnic or social identity, and transnationalism. Those studies of speech play that do exist tend not to analyze linguistic detail, even in places like Bali, where speech play is a cultural focus of considerable significance (as has been noted in passing by many scholars who have carried out research on this Indonesian island). Contemporary writing in both literary criticism and anthropology, from poststructuralist and postmodern perspectives, considers the concept of play as central to its enterprise, but, once again, rarely provides extended and detailed linguistic analysis of specific forms. In contrast, a linguistic orientation and detailed linguistic analysis are central to my project. At the same time, my approach is relevant to poststructuralist and postmodern concerns.

The study of speech play is relevant to ethnography in several ways. Play is often a cultural and linguistic theme, located in both grammar and culture. In fact, through testing, experimenting with, and sometimes creating the boundaries of appropriate behavior, it is often at the heart of intersections among language, culture, society, and individual expression. While there is always some play for play's sake, play often involves culture exploring and working out both its essence and the limits of its possibilities. In this view, language and culture and their interaction and intersection are dynamic, not static, and in flux, not fixed. The study of people's speech play gives us a glimpse of their coming to terms with their language and culture and is therefore a means of our coming to terms with their language and culture.

Like speech play and humor, verbal art has not entered anthropology's canon of major research topics. Yet its study has figured prominently in the development of one subfield of anthropology, linguistic anthropology, and especially the approach that has come to be known as the ethnography of speaking. The ethnography of speaking studies the relationships between language and culture and language and society from an ethnographic perspective. Empirical analyses of actual instances of language use, derived from extended field research, are related to native cultural conceptions and practices of speaking. Much work in the ethnography of speaking, including my own, has become increasingly discourse-centered and, especially, has focused on verbally artistic performances of myths, stories, and magical chants, as well as everyday conversations.[13] One offshoot of the ethnography of speaking is ethnopoetics—the representation, translation, and analysis of verbal art. Research in ethnopoetics is central to my approach to speech play and verbal art.[14]

While linguistic analysis is also basic to my approach, the discipline of linguistics, like the disciplines of anthropology and literature, has marginalized and trivialized the study of play, though with some significant, mainly methodological exceptions. And yet speech play, as I conceive it, is critically relevant to linguistics. It enables me to deal with not only standard topics in the study of the grammars of languages but also and especially topics which are salient for the speakers of particular languages—for example, the orientation to and focus on form, shape, texture, movement, position, and direction in Kuna, or sound symbolism and onomatopoeia in both Kuna and Balinese. My orientation to speech play also leads me to recognize, indeed insist on, alternative rather than unitary solutions to analytical problems such as the underlying representation of the sound patterns of a language. More generally, my approach argues for a plurality of theories and methods, an openness to different ways of conceiving of language and to different ways of collecting and analyzing data. Finally, attention to speech play and verbal art forces me to pay much more serious attention to issues of representation and translation of instances and forms of language use (discourse), especially oral forms, than is customary in linguistics.

The study of speech play is relevant to the understanding of the nature of language in general, since play is an important component of language structure and language use. Speech play also offers insights into particular languages, indicating what parts are available for play, and how and why they are available. Methodologically, speech play is a valuable tool for the investigation of both language structure and language use, revealing the ways in which various elements of language can be manipulated in different contexts. From the perspective of sociolinguistics, since speech play often emerges from languages, styles, and varieties in contact, its study provides insights into the use of and attitudes towards the sociolinguistic repertoire of a community.[15]

My theoretical perspective in this book is that of a sociolinguistically informed, discourse-centered, ethnographic approach to language structure and language use. This contributes to and is indeed a logical continuation of the Boas-Sapir-Whorf tradition in anthropology and linguistics with regard to the relationship between language and culture—that is, linguistic structures on the one hand and worldview or perception on the other. While Boas, Sapir, and their students considered the writing down of texts to be an essential part of linguistic fieldwork and analysis, these texts tended not to be studied as verbal art and were not viewed as the place to look for intersections between language and culture. Rather, the Sapir-Whorf hypothesis, as it has come to be known, is traditionally associated with a search for isomorphisms between grammar, conceived of in a narrow, abstract sense, and culture, conceived of as a separate, nonverbal entity. According to my approach, however, some aspects of linguistic form and linguistic structure only emerge through the study of language use in verbally playful and verbally artistic discourse. In fact, speech play and verbal art involve language in its essence, on display. Potentials inherent in language are packed and pushed to their highest limits. Playfully imaginative and artistically creative language constitutes the richest point of intersection between language, culture, society, and individual expression and therefore the place in which language, cognition, perception, and worldview come together in their most distilled form. Heteroglossia (languages, dialects, and speech styles in contact and competition within communities) and intertextuality (various kinds of combinations of forms of discourse) can be both sources of play and results of play.[16]

While many forms of speech play and verbal art are quite widespread and can be analyzed in terms of general cross-cultural dimensions, it is ultimately particular communities, cultures, and individuals who define speech play and verbal art, by talking about it, by using it, and by performing it. And it is the task of ethnography to approach speech play and verbal art from these local, community-based definitions and enactments.

Juxtapositions of items that intertextually surprise, arouse, enlighten, annoy, or challenge readers and observers constitute a major form of the postmodern experience. I feel it to be quite appropriate, then, that I have juxtaposed and indeed loosely coupled so many different verbal forms in this book—puns, jokes, riddles, limericks, verbal dueling, proverbs, play languages, code switching, trickster tales, palindromes, anagrams, song lyrics, traditional indigenous chants, and modern European poetry. I consider these juxtapositions of different forms of verbal play, creating play out of play, to be one of my contributions to the aesthetics as well as the politics of play.

My focus on play, the way I conceive of it, fits well within current conceptions of discourse and culture (and I would add language) as constructed, imagined, negotiated, interpreted, (re)invented, and subverted. Instead of viewing language and culture as systems where everything holds together nicely and neatly, I see them as open systems with squishes, fuzziness, leaks, inventions, constructions, negotiations, and imaginations, and as constantly emergent. Discourse is crucial to the language-and-culture intersection, the locus of the actualization of potentials provided by both language and culture as well as personal experience. In this intersection, creativity, imagination, and play are essential. Another way to view this is that there is a lack of fit between words and world, so that while at times language reflects the world, it often creates experience and perception. Again, speech play and verbal art are at the heart of this process, and they help us to understand not only relationships among language, culture, and thought but also the creative spirit which constantly inspires new forms of expression and aesthetic creation.

We enter the twenty-first century with a complex of theoretical and methodological approaches to language and culture and their intersection, all of which are relevant to this book—structural linguistics, generative linguistics, and sociolinguistics; cognitive, interpretive, and dialogic anthropology; and the ethnography of speaking and communication, poststructuralism, and postmodernism. I offer here a detailed description and analysis of forms, processes, and patterns of speech play and verbal art, in terms of linguistic structures and performance parameters as well as cross-cultural and ethnographic contexts. I also propose a positioning of these forms, processes, patterns, and contexts, sometimes as expressions (and manipulations and negotiations) of status or identity, sometimes of authenticity, sometimes of change and adaptation, sometimes of hegemony or deference to hegemony, sometimes of counterhegemony and resistance, sometimes of resistance to resistance.

I intend for this book to be simultaneously theoretical, scholarly, interesting, playful, and fun(ny). Easy to say but not always easy to do. And as interesting, engaging, or humorous as each form of speech play might be in and for itself, my point is to show that when these different kinds of materials from different places are brought together and integrated with illustrative examples, analyzed in linguistic detail, and socially, culturally, and interactionally contextualized, they make a forceful argument for the significance of speech play (in conjunction with verbal art) in anthropology and linguistics.

CHAPTER 2

The Grammar of Play
and the Play of Grammar

All grammars leak
—Edward Sapir, *Language*

Language in general and languages in particular are structured as open systems, flexible and creative. Every element of language and, especially, the relations between elements provide potentials for forms, processes, and patterns of speech play and verbal art. These are exploited in communities around the world as part of the give-and-take of everyday verbal interaction as well as in focused and highlighted performances.

Speech play and verbal art are both inherent and potential in language because of certain features of language that have long been noticed by linguists but rarely interpreted as I interpret them here.

In general, language is a relationship between sound (or gestures or written signs) and meaning. A basic principle of the expression of this sound-meaning relationship is the distinction between *signifiant* 'signifier' and *signifié* 'signified,' including the double aspect of the signified, denotation and connotation. Speech play can be based on signifiers, on signifieds, or on their relationship. Play based on signifiers includes rhyme, assonance, and alliteration. Play based on signifieds includes figures of speech, especially those involving comparison such as metaphor and metonym. Play based on the relationship between signifiers and signifieds includes puns, sound symbolism and onomatopoeia, and visually shaped poetry.

Another basic principle of language structure is the distinction between a paradigmatic axis of choice, which is potential, virtual, and implicit, and a syntagmatic axis of arrangement, which is overt, actual, and explicit.[1] The interplay of the paradigmatic and syntagmatic axes enables speech play and verbal art of many kinds, including puns, verbal dueling, and parallelism.

Still another way to view the relationship between language structure and speech play and verbal art is to notice that language structure and language use involve a constant interplay of sames and differences (repetitions and contrasts) at several levels simultaneously—sounds (consonants and vowels), syllables, syntactic units (noun phrases and verb phrases), semantic units of various kinds, pauses in the flow of speech, and speech acts (greetings, leave-takings, thank-yous, acknowledgments of thank-yous, questions, answers, requests, and commands). In addition to whatever information about referential content that is expressed through the patterned use of these sames and differences, this interplay also provides for various possibilities for speech play and verbal art that go beyond grammar, as they can be manipulated in many ways (for example, in poetry).

All languages are organized in terms of a number of components and levels, most recently called *modules*. These are sound patterns (phonetics and phonology), word structure (morphology), sentence structure (syntax), semantics, and discourse. These modules are loosely coupled together, in that each has a structure of its own and leads a semi-independent existence from the others. This loose linking of modules is precisely one of the meanings of play I presented in Chapter 1, and is one aspect of what Sapir had in mind with his very provocative statement, "All grammars leak" (1921: 38). And it is what enables such verbally playful and artistic processes as the stretching and manipulation of grammar and the overlapping and interpenetration of grammatical categories.

Every grammar provides a set of rules within which, instead of rigorous, tight consistency, there is considerable freedom—that is, considerable play. There are often many ways to express the same idea. Pronunciation, morphosyntax, and semantics can be varied. A good example of this is what traditional grammar terms *irregularity*. Thus, the regular English noun plural is formed by suffixing -s, -z, -es, or -ez (cats, dogs, etc.). Yet there are also irregular forms which do not follow this pattern but use others instead (oxen, mice, etc.). Similarly, the regular past tense of verbs is formed by suffixing -ed (worked), but irregular patterns exist as well (ate, came). The French regular noun plural is formed by suffixing -s (livres 'books'), but irregular forms also exist (oeil 'eye,' yeux 'eyes'). Spanish has two regular past-tense verb forms, as in compré 'I bought' and comí 'I ate.' But it also has irregular patterns, as in fui 'I went' and tuve 'I had.'

Loose coupling also occurs between meaning (semantics) in a language and the formal expression of meaning. Thus in English the prefix *un-* expresses the meaning of logical opposite in adjectives and verbs, as in *unbelievable* and *undo*. But *un-* is also prefixed in cases where the notion of logical opposite is not so obvious or even present, as in *uncanny*, *untold*, and *unfurl*. Similarly, prepositions in English are used to express meanings having to do with location and direction (sit in the house, walk up the stairs), but are also used for a variety of other meanings (eat up the food, write down the answer). In Kuna, with regard to counting, numeral classifiers are used, and these typically correspond to the form and shape of the object being counted. But sometimes they do not, as when the classifier *kwa* 'round object' is used to count houses, even if they are large and square.

These inconsistencies and irregularities in form-meaning relationships are actually instances of linguistic competition and play, and they are often sources of humor for children as they learn them and resources for verbal artists as they exploit them. Similarly, every grammar produces ambiguities in form-meaning relationships. A famous example from the history of linguistics is the sentence *Flying planes can be dangerous*, in which what is dangerous can be either the planes or the act of flying them. In Kuna the sentence *Pedro ur mai tanikki* can have many meanings, including, but not limited to, 'Pedro's boat is coming,' 'Someone or something is coming under Pedro,' 'Pedro is coming to paint the boat,' and 'Someone is coming to paint Pedro's boat.' Like irregularity, ambiguity is an example of grammar leaking and is a source of play, humor, and verbal artistry.

Speech Play and Verbal Art in Grammar, or The Linguistic Sign Is Not Arbitrary

Peircean semiotics teaches us that there are three kinds of sign: symbols, icons, and indexes.[2] Symbols are arbitrary signs, in which the relationship between sound and meaning is established by convention. Icons are signs in which the relationship between sound and meaning is motivated and seems natural. Indexes are signs which indicate or point to their referent, as a finger does in a pointing-hand gesture. Examples of indexes in language are the grammatical categories of person and tense. While the boundaries between and among these three types of sign are useful, in actual practice, and especially when language is viewed in its social and cultural context, these boundaries are slippery, overlapping, and intersecting—that is, they involve play. Once we recognize this we can happily break with the notion that linguistic signs are purely arbitrary. Indeed, the idea of arbitrariness is itself a resource for play.

Iconicity

Iconicity in language, including in particular such manifestations as sound symbolism/onomatopoeia and reduplication, is an old and somewhat controversial topic in linguistics. My intention here is to provide a new perspective on this discussion, within a more general framework of speech play and verbal art. This moves us from the tradition, from Saussure to Chomsky, that views linguistic forms, processes, and rules as arbitrary and formal to the tradition, from Sapir to Whorf to Jakobson to contemporary linguistic anthropologists, that views them as iconic and indexical, motivated in social, cultural, and aesthetic contexts.

I begin with the expression of three basic grammatical categories: number, tense, and aspect. Each of these, almost universally, adds on something to a word—to indicate more than one, in the case of number; to express distance from the present, the here and now, in the case of tense; and to differentiate repetition or duration from a single action or moment, in the case of aspect. This adding on, whether done by affixes, reduplication, or periphrastically, is iconic in that a grammatical adding on expresses a semantic adding on. Here are some examples:

	Number	
Language	Singular	Plural
English	book	book-s
	child	child-ren
Kuna	*machi* 'boy'	*machi-mala* 'boys'
	tat 'grandfather'	*tat-kan* 'grandfathers'
Indonesian	*buku* 'book'	*buku-buku* 'books'

	Tense	
	Present	Past or Future
English	work	work-ed, will work
Spanish	*come* 'eats'	*com-ió* 'ate'
		comerá 'will eat'

	Aspect	
English	eat	is/was eating
French	*mange* 'eats'	*mang-eait* 'is/was eating'
Nahuatl	*teki* 'cut'	*te?teki* 'cut into pieces'

SOUND SYMBOLISM

Probably the most commonly considered cases of iconicity in language are sound symbolism/onomatopoeia and reduplication, sometimes found in combination. Both sound symbolism and reduplication are manifested in different ways in different languages. I begin with sound symbolism.

In English, sound symbolism is almost grammaticalized, given the large number of words with initial *sn* or *sl*, which are sound sequences that seem like initial morphemes with actual meanings. Examples include *sniff, snooty, snout, snipe, snide, sneak, snort, snarl, snoop, slippery, slide, slimy, slither.*

In some languages, sound symbolism is a core part of the grammar. Thus in many indigenous languages of western North America, there is a shift in the place and manner of articulation of consonants according to the size of an object described and/or the speaker's attitude toward the object.[3] Sounds which are higher, further front in the mouth, and unvoiced symbolize diminutive, while sounds which are lower, further back in the mouth, and voiced symbolize augmentative. A good example comes from Wishram Chinook, where an object in its normal size with a *sh* or *ch* sound is pronounced in its diminutive size with an *s* or *c* (*ts*) sound and in its augmentative size with a *z* (*dz*) or *zh* sound. Thus *ch'iau* 'snake,' *c'iau* 'small snake,' and *zhiau* 'big snake.'[4] In Nootka, analogous sound symbolism is used to express the speech of certain characters or categories of person in performed narratives, thus providing a very good example of the intimate relationship between grammar, speech play, and sociolinguistics.[5] Examples include suffixing -*is* to nouns and verbs when talking to or about a child and suffixing -*aq* when talking to or about people who are fat.

Sound symbolism can be an aspect of a morphological process or pattern, as in the Spanish diminutive and augmentative suffixes -*ito*, -*ico*, -*illo* and -*aco*, -*azo*, -*ote*, -*ón*, which indicate both actual size and sociolinguistic affect, as do the Italian -*ino* and -*accio*. In these examples, an *i* sound expresses smallness and an *a* or *o* sound expresses largeness. This same vocalic contrast, *i/o* or *a*, is found between the Nahuatl respect suffix -*tzin* and diminutive suffix -*pil*, which also indicates endearment, on the one hand, and the diminutive but pejorative suffix -*toon* and pejorative suffix -*pool*, on the other.

Sometimes it is a single word which is sound symbolic, like Indonesian *emplung* 'to drop into the water,' the Chinese reduplicated form *ping pang* 'rattling of rain on the roof,' or English *thunk* or *buzz*. Expressive and emotive words like *shshsh* are typically sound symbolic. Often sets of words in particular semantic domains, such as the names for animals and the calls they make, are sound symbolic. Thus English *cuckoo, oink, meow;* French *cocorico* (for the sound a cock makes), *aboie* 'bark'; Balinese *meguek* 'pig squeals,' *guék-guék* 'squeal of pig,' *mekiak-kiak* 'chick chirps,' *kiak-kiak* 'chirp of chick.'

Finally there is the onomatopoeia and sound symbolism that poets, both oral and literate, exploit and even create, thus developing in discourse a form/semantic relationship, so that meanings like size, texture, movement, and shape seem naturally related to the sounds that describe them. Put another way—which is consistent with my view of speech play more generally—sound symbolism is a potential in language, which is actualized in discourse, especially verbally artistic discourse.[6]

REDUPLICATION

Reduplication is the multiple (usually double) occurrence of a sound string, syllable, morpheme, word, or phrase, usually but not necessarily contrasting with a single occurrence. Considerable attention has been devoted to both the forms and the meanings/functions of reduplication, which is often used as an example (perhaps the best) of a grammatical/semantic process which directly and obviously connects sound and meaning. There is considerable cross-linguistic consistency in the meaning and function of reduplication, including plurality—especially distributive, repeated, or continued occurrence; reciprocity; intensity; custom; and attenuation. Reduplication is particularly characteristic of certain registers, such as baby/caretaker talk, the language of respect as well as insult, and emotive language. Interestingly, it is used to express such opposites as augmentation and diminution or endearment and contempt, often in the same language. It is often felt to be playful, even humorous and/or aesthetically pleasing, and is related to parallelism, the basic underlying principle of poetry. It is frequent in pidgin and creole languages and may provide insights into the origin and evolution of language.

While reduplication is extremely widespread and most likely universal, its properties, including its form/function/meaning relationships, vary typologically. Here are some examples from four languages that differ from one another geographically, typologically, and in terms of their genetic relationship: English (with some comparative examples from French and Spanish), classical Nahuatl, Kuna, and Balinese.

Reduplication is not part of the formal grammar of English, French, or Spanish. Yet it occurs in baby talk and endearment talk and is used, somewhat playfully and humorously, to indicate such notions as intensity and true or core meaning.

ENGLISH
bye-bye, choo choo
many many thanks; very very strong
win-win situation
it's a no-no
same old same old

fast but not fast fast (= overly fast)

quick quick questions (= very quick)

She had some roast beef, some cheese, some crackers. She really ate ate (= ate a lot of food).

I'm gonna get my hair cut short short (= really short).

I haven't been so angry for a long long time.

In June we were not busy busy but busy (= not real busy, but somewhat so).

One person says to another, "Oh he's coming soon." The other responds, "Oh not soon soon."

coffee coffee (= black, without cream or sugar)

hot hot (= temperature wise, not spicy wise)

teacher teacher (= in a school, not a ski or tennis instructor)

My parents were friendly with George. Not close close but friendly.

A visitor to an office in a large New York City building asks the receptionist how to get out of the office. She responds, "Do you mean out out?" (= out of this particular office and also all the way out to the street)

(said by a Korean American) I recently became friends with Korean Koreans and I've become aware of how different Korean Koreans are.

FRENCH

cache cache 'hide and seek'

très très bien 'very very good'

Sa mère est metisse. Sa grandmère est noir noir. 'His mother is a half-breed. His grandmother is really black.'

Vous ne pouvez téléphonez qu'a Paris Paris (= within Paris city limits, not in the suburbs)

Il faut tourner a gauche gauche (= completely left, not slightly left)

SPANISH

ya ya 'OK OK'

bueno bueno 'good good' (both with ironic affect)

A man tells a woman that he is going to a fiesta where there will be a *toro* 'bull' dancing. She responds that it will be the cardboard bull mask that people wear in processions. He responds that this time there will be a live bull and she says, "Oh, you mean a *toro toro*" (= a real bull).

According to a verbal pattern found in Northern Mexican Spanish (which affects a small set of verbs), the verb is reduplicated in a subjunctive or quasi-subjunctive form, with the meaning, in a playful sense, of duration or repetition. Examples are:

> *llori llori* 'crying a lot' (from *llorar* 'cry'), as in *estoy llori llori* 'I am all tears'; *cante cante* 'sings a lot' (from *cantar* 'sing'), as in *empieza a cante cante* 'he begins to sing'; *baile baile* 'dances a lot' (from *bailar* 'dance'); *tiemble tiemble* 'trembling, shivering a lot' (from *temblar* 'tremble'); *güiri güiri* 'squeal,' 'chatter,' or 'babble' (no unreduplicated form, but perhaps related to *guiri-gay* 'gibberish' (an appropriate English translation might be 'yackety yak').

A nonsubjunctive case is *llueve llueve* 'rains a lot' (from *llover* 'rain'), as in *estuvo llueve llueve* 'it was constantly drizzling.' Notice the French word

> coupe coupe 'machete'

which exists alongside the word *machete* and is of probable Pidgin/creole French origin. A methodological aside is relevant here. These English, French, and Spanish examples were all taken from natural speech. I do not believe that intuited examples or invented examples are appropriate to the investigation of the kind of speech play and speech play/grammatical interplay I am exploring here. This point leads me to my next example, which I recorded from an excellent narrator of stories in Austin, Texas.[7]

> he (an animal) is standing there sniffing the ground sniffing the ground (keeps doing it here and there)

Notice the resemblance of this example (in function, not form) to the Amerindian verbal aspectual pattern described below. It signifies that the animal is continuously sniffing here and there.

As in some of the Kuna examples, English reduplication can be multiple.

> Housing prices are local local local.
> It's in the beginning beginning beginning stages.
> There's been a lot a lot a lot of that.
> It takes hours and hours and hours of time.
> What do real-estate agents consider the most important criterion for a home?: Location location location.

Can you give me a brief presentation? Brief brief brief.

They only come for an emergency emergency emergency.

I have two kids in college. So I'm workin' workin' workin'.

Young man says to young woman on campus (both university students): "I'll call you tonight and tell you about it." She responds: "Yes please please please call me."

People come in here if they really really really really want to climb the fence.

Two days ago the owners made what they thought was their final final final final final final offer.

Reduplication in English is also related to an enormous group of very playful vocabulary items which take the form of doublets.

flimflam, hurly-burly, itsy-bitsy, wishy-washy, pitter-patter, singsong, willy-nilly, roly-poly, riffraff

In English, French, and Spanish, reduplication clearly enters significantly into the expressive, playful, and humorous aspect of language use. It can be a source or focus of aesthetics or humor, as in these Spanish songs and jokes.

Tendrás que llorar y llorar y llorar y llorar y llorar y llorar.
Tendrás que buscar y buscar y buscar y buscar y buscar y buscar.
'You have to cry and cry and cry and cry and cry and cry.'
'You have to search and search and search and search and search and search.'[8]

Question: Por qué no nada nada? 'Why don't you swim worth a damn?'
Answer: Porque no traje traje. 'Because I didn't bring my bathing suit.'

Question (Spaniard asks German): Where are you from?
Answer: Baden Baden. And where are you from?
Answer: San Lucar de Barrameda San Lucar de Barrameda.

Nahuatl, the language of the Aztecs and their descendants, exhibits a pattern found in many (but not all) indigenous languages of North America, in particular the widespread Uto-Aztecan family.[9] Reduplication of the initial consonant (if any) and the following vowel, with insertion of a glottal stop in nominal and adjectival stems, is a productive grammatical process used to indicate a distributive plural.

teotl 'god,' *teʔteo* 'gods here and there'
kowatl 'snake,' *koʔkowa* 'snakes here and there'
kwalli 'good,' *kwalzin* 'good, with respect,' *kwaʔkwalzin* 'good,
    with intense respect'

In verbs, reduplication of the initial consonant (if any) and the following vowel is used to express an intensive, habitual, or continuous, action.

chooka 'to weep,' *choochooka* 'to weep loudly'
teki 'to cut with a knife,' *teteki* 'to slice'

The same reduplication pattern, with an inserted glottal stop, expresses a distributive or interrupted repetitive action.

teki 'to cut with a knife,' *teʔteki* 'to cut into pieces'

Notice how the same verb, *teki*, enters into two different patterns of reduplication, resulting in two different meanings. A doubling of the glottal reduplication pattern (actually a double reduplication) expresses an intensification of the repetitive notion.

nemi 'to walk,' *neʔneʔnemi* 'to walk up and down, stopping inter-
    mittently'

Yet how grammatically productive is this pattern? It seems similar to other languages, such as Balinese, in which a grammatically productive reduplication pattern is extended for playful and expressive purposes.

In addition to the reduplication of roots or stems, diminutive, augmentative, endearing, and derogatory suffixes can be reduplicated, giving more intensity to the affect expressed by these suffixes as well as indicating distributive plurality.

siwatl 'woman,' *siwapil* 'little/fine woman,' *siwapilpil* 'little/fine
    women here and there'; *piltontli* 'son,' *pilpiltonton* 'sons here and
    there'

Notice the reduplication of both the stem and the affix in *pilpiltonton*. In this last set of examples, as I believe may also be the case in the previous set, the grammatical/referential function of reduplication blends into or is extended into an expressive function.

In Kuna, reduplication is not a very productive grammatical process, but it does have some grammatical functioning. Three of the four verbal positional suffixes can be reduplicated to indicate a distributive plural.

tule seretkus purkwenanai 'many old people are dying right now'
(the suffix -*nai* 'ongoing in a perched position' is partially
reduplicated)

saklakan kaski mamai 'the chiefs are distributed here and there in
hammocks' (the suffix -*mai* 'ongoing in a horizontal position' is
partially reduplicated)

Somewhat productive is a pattern of total reduplication of adjectives,
to indicate distribution.

korokwa 'ripe,' *korokorokwa* 'various are ripe'
warrakwa 'wet,' *warrawarrakwa* 'various are wet'

Certain adjectives—for example, those describing form and color—
can be reduplicated, expressing distribution in space.

murru 'hill, bump,' *murru murru* 'bumpy, like the skin of a caiman'
sip(p)u 'white,' *kakkula sip sip sii* 'his lips are spotted white'[10]

Certain adverbs are reduplicated to indicate intensity. This pattern is
similar to English *very very* or *many many*, though it seems to be a more
productive process in Kuna and extends beyond pure intensity.

kwae 'fast,' *kwae kwae* 'very fast'
pane 'tomorrow,' *pane pane* 'every day'
kwen(a) 'one,' *kwena kwenakwa* 'some'
muchup 'reciprocally,' *muchup muchup sae* 'do reciprocally'

A large set of reduplicated adjectives, some of which are derived from
nouns or verbs and many of which do not occur in unreduplicated form,
describe in fine detail the form and shape of objects. These words are
playful, aesthetic, and affective. They constitute a specialized vocabulary not common in either everyday or formal and ritual speech, and
they are known only to certain, usually older and traditionally oriented
individuals.

purwikwa 'small,' *purwipurwikwa* 'in small pieces'
sinni 'curl,' *sinnisinnikwa* 'all curled up'
ukka 'skin, bark,' *ukka ukka* 'having pieces of skin or bark
    peeling off'
iti iti 'jagged'

sirpi sirpi 'having close circular lines, as around a tree or pole'
sili sili 'having fairly widely separated circular lines, as around a
    tree or pole'

This last group of examples, although from a very large set, are somewhat esoteric. I have mainly been able to learn about them from elicita-
tion, tapping into the competence of speakers who know them. I have
rarely heard them in everyday speech or found them in recorded performances. On the other hand, all of the other examples are quite common, in both everyday speech and in verbally artistic performances.
Here is a final set of Kuna words which are reduplicated several times, a
pattern quite commonly used as a humorous, expressive, onomatopoetic device in narrative performances.

apparmaysi apparmaysi apparmaysi appar oallenatappi ikarpal
    'running running running run laughing along down the path'[11]
natap natap natap natap natap 'they go along they go along they go
    along they go along they go along'[12]
irki irki irki tiki enuynasunnat 'rubbing rubbing rubbing to clean
    them (his paws) in the water'

Balinese shares with other Indonesian languages the very productive
use of reduplication as a grammatical process, to indicate plurality, repetition, and intensity, among other meanings. For plurality:

High Balinese: *ayam* 'chicken,' *ayam ayamé akéh* 'many chickens'
Ordinary Balinese: *siap* 'chicken,' *siap siapé liu* 'many chickens'

For repetition and intensity:

nawah 'bargain,' *nawah nawah* 'keep bargaining'

For a play version of something or playing at something:

High Balinese: *kolem* 'sleep,' *mekolem koleman* 'pretend to sleep'
Ordinary Balinese: *sirep* 'sleep,' *sirep sirepan* 'pretend to sleep';
    pules 'sleep,' *pules pulesan* 'pretend to sleep'

For names of things that don't have nonreduplicated names:

pici pici 'squid'

In addition, reduplication is highly developed in the Balinese iconic, onomatopoetic, and playful/humorous vocabulary. Here are some examples in which vowel shifts are combined with reduplication.

sliak sliuk 'go up and down'
delak delik 'stare angrily' (as Balinese dancers do when they pause momentarily and look at the audience)
dengak dengok 'look around in different directions'
ungkal angkil 'boisterously'
kilak kiluk 'zigzag'

Names for animals and the sounds they make are particularly good examples of the playful and expressive use of reduplication combined with the sound symbolism of consonant and vowel combinations and changes.

cuit cuit 'the squeaking of a mouse'
pecat pecit 'chirping of a bird'
pecit pecit 'sound of a baby bird'
bébék 'duck,' ngegék gék 'quack'
ceruet ceruet 'cry of monkey'
ngongkong 'bow of dog'
meguék guék 'oink of pig'

While seemingly central to some languages and marginal to others, reduplication, like sound symbolism more generally, can be seen as an important aspect of all languages when language is viewed in sociocultural context and when the playful and aesthetic functions of language are considered to be as important as the expression of reference. Reduplication is a manifestation of the iconic, sound-symbolic, and play potential of language. As reflected in the examples I have presented here, it can be found in two different areas of language use (with typological variations around the world): on the one hand, in grammar, where over time it seems to get more and more integrated, more and more formally arbitrary, and less and less obviously iconic, and, on the other hand, in playfully aesthetic, expressive, and affective language. In some instances these two areas seem to blend into one another, raising questions about the boundaries of grammar and discourse and the boundaries of formal referentiality and aesthetic play.

Since reduplication is a type of patterned repetition, it is, potentially or actually, intimately related to the poetic function of language, which Jakobson and others have defined in terms of patterns or systems of repetition. And the ways in which reduplication moves across the boundaries of the grammatical/referential function of language and the playful/aesthetic functions of language fit quite nicely within Jakobson's very apt conceptualization of the relationship between linguistic structures and the aesthetics of language—"the poetry of grammar and the grammar of poetry."[13] It is also noteworthy that while reduplication is often found in special, seemingly marginal areas of language use and is not immediately accessible to nonnative speakers or outside investigators, it is also very characteristic of a language, reflecting its basic feel or form. There is something very English about *hurly-burly*, something very Balinese about *delak delik*.

Finally, it is important to note that reduplication is characteristic of baby/caretaker talk, pidgins and creoles, and affective language, adding support to those who believe that there is a relationship among these registers, styles, and varieties of language which sheds light on the origin and evolution of language.[14]

As overwhelmingly formal and foreboding a structure as grammar is, as any linguist or student of a foreign language well knows, there is also play, and indeed humor and art, right at its core, as I have illustrated here. Play and art are both inherent and potential in linguistic structure; they are an important part of what language is all about. The implications and consequences of this situation will be developed in subsequent chapters.

CHAPTER 3

Forms of Speech Play in Context

Eechspay ayplay andhay erbalvay arthay

Brevity is the soul of wit.   —Shakespeare, *Hamlet*

Two guys walk into a bar and the third one ducks.

What walks with four legs in the morning,
two at noon, and three in the evening?   (Answer: Man)

Play languages, puns, jokes, put-ons, proverbs, riddles, and verbal dueling are extremely widespread in the world. They are often recognized, named, codified, and evaluated. While collections of these forms abound and can be found in libraries, bookstores, and on the internet, my approach to them is unique in several ways. In addition to describing their formal verbal properties and organization, I place them in both ethnographic and interactional contexts, examining their social and cultural roles in different societies, as well as their strategic use in face-to-face dialogues and conversations. I also focus on their relationship to one another and to speech play and verbal art more generally.

Play Languages

Play languages are one of the most common forms of speech play. They are linguistic codes derived by a small set of rules from a language in use in a particular speech community. Scholars also call play languages *disguised speech, linguistic games, ludling, pig Latins, secret codes, secret languages,* and *speech disguise.* They are usually known by the names given to them by the people that speak them, names such as pig Latin, F language, talking backwards, or Abi Dabi. They have been reported in western European communities, in native and European-origin communities in North and South America, in Oceania, in Australia, and in Africa. They are usually based on manipulations of the sound patterns and structure of a language, but sometimes they are based on semantic structure as well. Although their rules are relatively simple, play languages disguise messages remarkably well.

The study of play languages is both theoretically and methodologically relevant to an analysis of linguistic structure. In the movement of sounds and syllables within words and the insertion of sounds and sound sequences, phonological structures, patterns, and strategies are revealed.[1] Here are some examples.

From English

Pig Latin moves the first sound or sound sequence of a word to the end of the word and then inserts a final -*ay; h* is used to replace absent initial consonants in words beginning with vowels.

give > ivgay
stop > opstay
it > ithay
Give it to me > Ivgay ithay ootay iymay

Op Language or Abi Dabi inserts -*op* inside every syllable:

Give it to me > Gopive opit topo mope

From Tobago creole

Giberidge 'gibberish' inserts *p* after every syllable followed by a vowel which copies or echoes the vowel of the syllable:

Don > dopon
Wendel > wependepel

From French

French offers a particularly interesting set of play languages. *Parler à l'envers* 'Speak backwards' reverses the order of the first two consonants or consonant clusters of a word or pair of words:

Passe moi la bouteille 'Pass me the bottle' > *Sap moi la toubeille*

Verlan (*l'envers* 'backwards' said backwards), the most contemporary of French play languages, reverses syllables, pronounces words backwards, and/or reverses the order of the first two consonants or consonant clusters of a word or pair of words:

Passe moi la bouteille > Sepas oim la teillebout
Tu est fous 'You are crazy' > T'est ouf

Il est mechant 'He is mean' > Il est chamer
Bonjour > Jourbon
Merci > Cimer

Verlan, while used by and associated with adolescents—in particular in certain lower-class and working-class suburbs of Paris—has become somewhat fashionable in France. In fact, many words from *verlan* have entered French *argot* 'slang,' and it is considered quite cool and "with it" for French youth to sprinkle their discourse with words from *verlan,* such as *Jourbon* and *Cimer.* The use of *verlan* is both intellectual and political. It can be found in songs, novels, and films, and there are *verlan* poetry sites on the internet.[2] To make matters even more complicated and interesting, the ways of deriving words in *verlan* are constantly changing. Individuals demonstrate how cool they are by using the latest derivations, for example *kemé* instead of *kem* (for the slang word *mec* 'guy'). And, based on *verlan,* a new play language has been invented in a southern suburb of Paris. It is called *veul* and is described as *verlan repassé au filtre du verlan* 'verlan passed through the filter of verlan' or *verlan*[2] 'verlan squared'. Thus *femme* 'woman' is *meuf* in *verlan* and *feume* in *veul; comme ça* 'like that' is *ça comme* in *verlan* and *asmeuk* in *veul.*

From Spanish

F language inserts *f* after every syllable followed by a vowel which copies or echoes the vowel of the syllable:

la casa grande 'the big house' > *lafa cafasafa grafandefe*

From Kuna

Talking backwards reverses the syllables of words:

merki pia pe nae 'American where are you going' > *kimer api pe ena*

Concealed talking inserts *pp* after every syllable followed by a vowel which copies or echoes the vowel of the syllable:

merki pia pe nae > *mepperkippi pippiappa peppe nappaeppe*

From Balinese

Secret language inserts *s* after every syllable followed by a vowel which copies or echoes the vowel of the syllable:

tiang ke peken 'I am going to the market' > *tisiasang kese pesekesen*

Play languages are used to mark ethnic and social identity, to keep secrets, and to express opposition to the hegemonic rule of upper-middle-class and education-oriented standard languages and dialects. They highlight speakers on display, showing off verbal virtuosity in an interactional, performance, and competitive mode. And, like all of the forms of speech play in this chapter, they can be used as pure play, simply for the fun of it.

Puns and Jokes

When approached in very general terms, puns and jokes are probably universal. But their structural properties and sociocultural and interactional patterning are different in particular languages, cultures, communities, and societies. While puns and jokes are often named forms in the communities in which they are found, there may not be total agreement on the precise definition of either the terms or the forms in actual usage.

Puns

In the most general terms, a pun is a form of speech play in which a word or phrase unexpectedly and simultaneously combines two unrelated meanings. Most English speakers, when they use the term *pun*, have in mind a form that is conscious, intended, and noticed. This is also the case with regard to related terms and forms in other European languages, such as French *jeu de mots* and *calembour*.[3] Some scholars, however, use the term *pun* for unintentional and unnoticed forms of word association that seem, in linguistic terms, to operate in ways quite similar to intended and conscious puns.[4]

Puns manipulate different levels and aspects of language, as shown by the following examples.

SOUND PATTERNS

(Said of a tennis player who was injured yet still playing very well)
Even crippled Burt is crippling.[5]
He took his team from the outhouse to the penthouse.[6]

And from the incessantly punning Marx brothers:

Butch: Keep out of this loft!
Chico: Well, it's better to have loft and lost than never to have loft at all.[7]

In this example, as is often the case with the Marx brothers' playful puns, it is not only sound patterns that are manipulated but imagined dialect differences as well (in this case the existence of dialects in which *loft* and *loved* are pronounced identically).

A quite similar example was observed in an everyday conversation:

I'm going to fish off the dock today, just for the halibut.

MORPHOLOGY AND LEXICON

Question: When is a door not a door?
Answer: When it's ajar.[8]

Question (asked of a native of the Caribbean island of Tobago): Are you from Tobago?
Answer: Born, bred, and buttered, get it?

This last pun is based on the homonyms *bred* and *bread*, as well as the proverbial expression "born and bred." Here are two from William Shakespeare, an exuberant user of puns.[9]

Sec. Com. I am but, as you would say, a cobbler.
Mar. But what trade art thou? answer me directly.
Sec. Com. A trade sir, that, I hope, I may use with a safe conscience; which is indeed, sir, a mender of bad soles.[10]

Mercutio [in *Romeo and Juliet*, talking about his own death]. Ask for me tomorrow and you shall find me a grave man.[11]

Again from the Marx brothers:

Mrs. Teasdale: Notables from every country are gathered here in your honor. This is a gala day for you.
Firefly: Well, a gal a day is enough for me. I don't think I could handle any more.[12]

SYNTAX AND SEMANTICS

A: Do you know how to sew on a button?
B: I think it's as easy as it seems.
A: Is that a seamstress joke? Very punny.[13]

I may have learned table manners growing up. I may have learned all manner of things.[14]

One of many Jewish jokes from the work of Sigmund Freud:

Two Jews met in the neighbourhood of the bath-house. "Have you taken a bath?" asked one of them. "What?" asked the other in return, "is there one missing?"[15]

PRAGMATICS

(Road sign indicating workers on the road) Working for you. Give us a brake.

You can call me whatever you want (= what name you want to), just don't call me late for dinner.[16]

And again from Shakespeare:

Polonius. What is the matter, my lord?
Hamlet. Between who?
Polonius. I mean the matter that you read, my lord.[17]

BILINGUAL PUNS

Puns based on the similarity of the words *dólares* 'dollars' and *dolores* 'pains, sorrows' are common among Mexican immigrants to the United States, and are very revealing of their painful experience in this country:

Me costó veinte dolores. 'It cost me twenty pains, sorrows.'

The most popular TV program in France in 2001 was *Loft story*, pronounced as if French, as well as punning on English *loft/love*.[18]

Puns relate to other discourse units, processes, and contexts in various ways. They can function both cohesively and disjunctively. They play a role in discourse cohesion in linking various utterances or parts of a discourse to each other. Puns often occur in proverbs and metaphors (which are related to the presentation of narrative material in conversation in that they often conclude it or sum it up as well as display understanding of it).[19] This is particularly the case with unintentional, unnoticed puns that are based on the fact that proverbial and idiomatic expressions can have both a literal and a figurative or more general interpretation.

> This chicken smells foul.
> This year we sent them fruitcake with pecans and they just went nuts over it.
> This girl comes into my class looking sour. I knew she was gonna be a lemon.[20]
> (Talking about a fire and what people can do when they have one in their house): Don't count on carrying your prized possessions with you in the heat of the moment.[21]
> Slavery's a black-and-white issue.[22]
> (Man talking about other suns being so bright that you could not see their planets): In light of that, the data were very scarce.[23]
> (Man who just lost his house in a flood, talking to reporters): We watched our lives, fifteen years of our life go down the drain.[24]
> So far there has been a drought in the international discussion about water.[25]
> We're stocking the Texas lakes with trout so we can get people hooked on fishing.[26]
> The players association made their pitch that John Rocker's penalty be overturned.[27]

Some observers might prefer the more neutral term *word association* for the phenomenon displayed in these examples, reserving the term *pun* for cases that are purposeful, noticed, and reacted to. But these examples have all the linguistic properties of purposeful puns and the same potential to be noticed and reacted to, or commented on, as in the following example:

> (A and B in conversation at a hotel breakfast table)
> A: How do you get your hair so nice?
> B: It's day by day with the curling iron.
> A: Keep plugging along.
> B: Keep plugging along. That's a good one.[28]

Puns can also function in exactly the opposite way. Instead of being cohesive, they can be disjunctive, breaking the frame of the discourse in which they are located.[29] This is often the result of intended, purposeful puns, such as the witty comebacks of conversation stoppers and the punch lines of jokes. Here is a conversation stopper, a very Groucho Marx–like example from French:

> (A and B are engaged in conversation and A says something B does
>   not understand)
> B: *hein?* (= 'what' but sounds like *un* = 'one')
> A: *deux* 'two' (as if they were counting)[30]

Puns can sometimes operate cohesively and disjunctively at the same time, as in work by the best literary punsters from Shakespeare to Joyce.

Puns may occur in rounds, uttered either by a single individual or by many. And they may be overtly framed in conventional ways. Conventional framings of and responses to puns, just like the form and structure of puns, vary in specific languages, cultures, and societies. In English, the best-known overt framing is probably the groan, produced by either the pun utterer or pun recipient—and which provides the term *groaner.* Another conventional way for pun makers to frame their puns is to use expressions such as "No pun intended" or "Excuse the pun."

> Given your, pardon the expression, crusty experience in bread
>   making.[31]

> (Student remarks): I was wondering if there was anything for me in
>   the archeology course and there was. Of course you gotta dig a
>   little.
> (Then he smiles and says): No pun intended.

These expressions, of course, insist on the cohesive rather than disjunctive functioning of puns. Still another conventional marker of a pun is laughter. At times an unconscious, unnoticed pun becomes noticed, either by the speaker or by a listener. Thus, by convention, it changes the nature of the discourse, which now focuses on the pun as if it were intended. This is precisely what happened during a public university lecture when the speaker said:

> Some things only happen to women. Period.

The lecturer apparently uttered this pun unwittingly. But when laughter erupted in the audience, she joined in.

From a sociological perspective we can view puns in terms of both social structure and social interaction. Social-structural issues involve such questions as, Who has the right to utter a pun to whom? Who has the right (or obligation) to overtly react to a pun uttered by certain others? In what contexts are puns most likely to be uttered or interpreted and reacted to? In social interactions, puns can be used by speakers or recipient-responders to display understanding of the presented narrative material. In addition, they can be used by speakers to obtain the floor in a conversation, change the topic, or relieve tension. The occurrence of a pun can also cause or result in social-interactional problems that must be attended to—that is, commented on, joked about, or apologized for.

Another perspective on puns is the ethnographic, which raises questions of cross-cultural comparison. There are differences in the linguistic structure of puns and related forms of speech play. For example, French and Spanish seem to allow much less phonetic and phonological manipulation in puns than does English, but the French-based creole languages of the Caribbean allow more manipulation than continental French. There are also differences in the role of puns in larger discourse patterns and structures (e.g., jokes, narratives, oratory), the topics for which puns are considered appropriate, and the attitudes toward puns and related behavior. In American white middle-class society, when discussing such taboo subjects as sex, individuals sometimes interpret as allusive puns words and phrases that would probably seem not at all punful to them if the discussion were about a nontaboo subject.[32] What makes a pun a pun, then, depends not only on properties purely internal to its structure nor even on the relationship between puns and the discourse in which they occur. Equally important are the topics dealt with within the discourse and such cross-culturally variable issues as whether the topic is taboo or whether it should be dealt with in direct speech or indirect, allusive speech.

There is also a historical dimension to attitudes toward puns and the appropriateness of pun usage. During certain periods in the English-speaking world, puns were considered to be high art and quite appropriate for serious topics. Today they are most often considered to be humorous in intention, inappropriate for serious discourse but highly appropriate for advertising.

The ways in which puns relate to more general communicative patterns in a society can also vary cross-culturally. While North American Indians and nearby white populations both use puns, for Indians puns are part of a pattern of kidding and teasing behavior that conflicts with non-Indian communicative behavior and can lead to misunderstandings in interactions between non-Indians and Indians—for example, in school classrooms. Here is an example from a school on the Warm Springs reservation in Oregon, in which the Anglo teacher ignores (or misses) the Indian student's clever pun, which occurs, inappropriately, from the teacher's point of view, during a serious class lesson.

> Teacher: What else smells good? [the correct answer is "flowers"]
> Student: Me.
> Student: My nose [students laugh].
> Teacher: All flowers smell good? [33]

The Kuna Indians of Panama rarely recognize or attend to puns in their own language. But on the other hand, they are extremely fond of word-association types of word play which hover between puns and metaphors. An example is the interactive, humorous riddle, in which one individual allusively names an object such as an animal for a second to guess. (See discussion of riddles below.)

Puns are often used in multilingual societies and situations. In Bali, incredibly complicated puns—which involve mixing the exuberant linguistic possibilities provided by the complex Balinese sociolinguistic system of speech levels, and sometimes the national language Indonesian, and even English and other tourist languages as well—are drawn on in the banter and joking of which the Balinese are forever fond, in both everyday conversation and ritual dance dramas and shadow-puppet plays. Here is an example based on the double meaning of the word *kuda*, which signifies 'how much?' in ordinary Balinese and 'horse' in both Indonesian and High Balinese:

> A (in Balinese, in a market stall): *Aji kuda?* 'How much?' (literally 'price how-much?')
> B *Aji jaran* (ordinary Balinese 'horse,' literally 'price horse')

It is interesting to note the way in which English, the language of tourism and the global economy, enters into the already existing cultural and verbal pattern of the punful comeback. Here are some examples involving the sound similarity between Balinese *siu* 'one thousand' and English *See you*. A person may say *Siu surat*, literally 'one thousand letter' but also a play on English *See you later*, in which Balinese and Indonesian *surat* 'letter' is a pun on English *later*. Or a person may say *Siu berjumpa*, with Indonesian *berjumpa* 'meet, see,' as if they were saying, multilingually, *See you see you*. A typically Balinese baroque and recherché leave-taking is *Siu satak*, literally 'one thousand two hundred.' Again this takes off from the similarity of Balinese *siu* and English *See you*. Added to this, however, is the fact that 'one thousand two hundred' can also be expressed as *nem bangsit*, literally 'six two hundred'—in which *bangsit*, with an *m/b* interchange, sounds like *mangsit* 'to stink.' This play, as is the case in many Balinese puns, is not on an uttered word but on an imagined or presupposed word.[34]

The best-known approach to puns, at least in the Western world, is probably the psychoanalytic, especially that developed by Freud in his study of wit in general. Freud stresses ambiguity and condensation in puns—the merger of several meanings, including unconscious meanings, into a single item. Freud also notes an aggressive component in both puns and jokes.[35] In fact, puns are speech play par excellence, foregrounding all that Freud noticed so perceptively but also other aspects of language and language use as well, including social-interactional strategies and competition; verbal deftness and quickness; social, cultural, and linguistic manipulations; and the creative pleasure of saying, hearing, and seeing what language can do.

Jokes

The term *joke* (and related terms in European languages such as *histoire drôle*, in French, and *chiste*, in Spanish) refers to a discourse unit consisting of two parts: the setup and the punch line. The punch line contains an element of surprise vis-à-vis the setup; it is this surprise relationship between the setup and the punch line that is the source of humor. The element of surprise typically involves an actualization of unstated assumptions of the setup, and "getting" or understanding the joke consists of relating the punch line to the unstated assumptions. In addition, the punch line often reframes the point of view established in the setup.[36] Seemingly simple, jokes involve complex manipulations of linguistic, interactional, and cultural relations. A lot is lurking behind them. There are a variety of types of jokes with regard to form, content, interactional properties, and performance.

RIDDLE JOKES

Riddle jokes are common among children but also found among adults. They consist of a question posed to a listener followed by an answer provided by the original questioner when, as is typically the case, the listener does not know it. Children's riddle jokes often use puns:

Question: How did Lassie feel after she ate some bad cantaloupe?
Answer: Melancholy.
Question: Why did the cookie visit the doctor?
Answer: He felt crummy.

Riddle and riddlelike jokes, like jokes with other structures, sometimes cluster around a particular topic; grapes, elephants, and light bulbs have become fads in this regard.

> Question: How do you shoot a pink elephant?
> Answer: With a pink-elephant gun.
> Question: How do you shoot a blue elephant?
> Answer: You dye it pink and shoot it with a pink-elephant gun.

> Question: How many football players does it take to screw in a light bulb?
> Answer: The entire team, and they get the semester off for it.[37]

Longer interactional-interrogative joke routines, such as the knock-knock jokes of American society that also often use puns, are found among children, and may be related to linguistic and communicative development—the acquisition of punning and joking abilities as well as competence in other forms of discourse.[38]

> Question: Why did the chicken cross the road?
> Answer: To get the *New York Times*, get it? Neither do I, I read the *Austin American-Statesman*.

Notice that this joke's first moment of humor is based on the presupposed knowledge of another children's joke:

> Question: Why did the chicken cross the road?
> Answer: To get to the other side.

Its second source of humor is the interactional victimizing of the recipient of the joke. In the following joke, the victim is a character (actually both characters) in the joke itself:

> A boy says to the teacher: "I want to go to the bathroom."
> The teacher says: "First you have to say the alphabet."
> So the boy says: "A, b, c, d, e, f, g, h, i, j, k, l, m, n, o, q, r, s, t, u, v, w, x, y, z."
> And the teacher says: "Where's the *p*?"
> The boy says: "Running down my leg."

Jokes which hinge on victimizing either characters within the joke or recipients of the joke are akin to trickster stories, and thus are part of a worldwide oral tradition.

Narrative jokes, common among adults, consist of a short narrative that ends in a surprising punch line. Like oral narratives generally, narrative jokes contain a series of actions and often include directly quoted, dramatized dialogue. Narrative jokes are much more laconically condensed and focused than ordinary narratives.

> A man was walking through Central Park, and he was stopped by a mugger. And he resisted. The mugger wanted to go through his pockets and he wouldn't let him. He resisted and the mugger beat him up badly. And finally he subdued him, went through his pockets, and found fifty-seven cents. So he said, "For fifty-seven cents you put up such a fight? You could've been killed." "Oh," the man said, "I didn't know you wanted the fifty-seven cents in my pocket. I thought you were after the two hundred dollars in my shoe."

> A guy is begging on the street and asks a man walking by for spare change. The man replies, "'Neither a borrower nor a lender be'— Shakespeare." To which the beggar replies, "'Fuck you'—Norman Mailer."

This joke uses a Shakespearean proverb in the quoted request, followed by a mock, proverbial-like quotation in the response, resulting in a mini verbal duel which is the centerpiece of the joke. (See the discussion of proverbs and verbal duels below.) For this book, a joke about a linguist is always appropriate:

> A distinguished linguistics professor was lecturing on the phenomenon of double negatives. As he neared the end of his talk, he drew himself up and declared solemnly, "In conclusion, let me observe that while there are numerous cases where a double negative conveys a positive, there is no case where a double positive conveys a negative." Whereupon, from the back of the room, arose a small voice dripping with disdainful condescension: "Yeah, yeah."

A common narrative-joke structure is tripartite or quadripartite, two or three actions setting up a pattern that is then broken by the surprising third or fourth action, which leads to or constitutes the punch line. While the punch line is the moment of a narrative joke considered to be the most funny and after which joke recipients are supposed to laugh, the material leading up to a punch line can also be funny and thus generate laughter, in part because of the expectation of the punch line.

> A priest was shipwrecked on a rock at low tide. Soon the water began rising, but luckily a rowboat appeared. The priest did not want to be taken on board, convinced that the Lord would help him. Soon the water rose to his hips, when a yacht approached. But the priest waved it off. When the water reached the priest's neck, a Coast Guard helicopter appeared. But he refused again, still counting on the Lord. When the priest drowned, he reproachfully confronted the Lord, asking why he had not been saved. "What do you mean?" the Lord answered, "Did I not send a row boat, a yacht, and a helicopter?"[39]

JOKES AND THE POLITICAL (UN)CONSCIOUS

Jokes often deal with contemporary themes, reflecting the events, attitudes, concerns, and indeed political unconscious of a moment.[40] Here is a joke Russians tell about their leaders, followed by a joke Americans tell about theirs.

> Brezhnev dies and is offered one of three tortures: First he sees Hitler in boiling water, then he sees Stalin on a rack, finally he sees Kruschev in bed with Brigitte Bardot. "I'll take that one," he says, "the one that Kruschev got." "No, that is Brigitte Bardot who is being tortured."[41]

> President Clinton and the Pope died on the same day, and, due to an administrative mix-up, Clinton was sent to heaven and the Pope went to hell. The Pope explained the situation to the Devil, who checked out all of the paperwork, and the error was acknowledged. The Pope was told, however, that it would take about twenty-four hours to correct the error. The next day, when the Pope was on his way up to heaven, he met Clinton on his way down, and they stopped to chat.
> Pope: "Sorry about the mix-up."
> Clinton: "No problem."
> Pope: "Well, I'm really excited about going to heaven."
> Clinton: "Why's that?"
> Pope: "All my life I've wanted to meet the Virgin Mary."
> Clinton: "Well, you're a day late."

Political jokes, like all jokes, involve an intense condensation of multiple presupposed meanings as well as some ambiguity of interpretation. Here is a particularly illustrative joke in this regard:

> Governor Wallace of Alabama died and went to heaven. After entering the pearly gates, he walked up to the door of a splendid mansion and knocked. A voice inside exclaimed, "Who dat?" Wallace shook his head sadly and said, "Never mind, I'll go the other way."[42]

Some of the meanings presupposed in this joke are the role of George Wallace as Mr. Racist/Segregationist in American society (especially in 1964 when this joke was recorded); wishful thinking (the death of the racist governor); the difference between heaven and hell and the idea that racists will eventually be punished by going to the latter, a form of self-inflicted punishment in this particular case; and the governance and peopling of heaven by blacks rather than whites, including the possibility that God and the apostles are black (all keyed[43] by the two-word utterance "Who dat?" which involves the basic intonational, phonological, and syntactic features of stereotypical Black English). Furthermore, the joke leaves ambiguous whether heaven is segregated (all black) or integrated (black and white) and whether the speaker is Saint Peter or a servant. In addition to the ambiguity, notice that this same joke could appear to be racist if told by a white person pejoratively making fun of African American English, mocking it as an inferior form of speech.[44]

Less ambiguous is a version of this joke I heard shortly after Wallace's death. I find this version less effective, both because of its relative lack of ambiguity and because it no longer uses (mock) African American English:

> George Wallace dies and goes to heaven. He gets to the pearly gates and sees that Saint Peter is black. Saint Peter says, "What can I help you with?" George Wallace says, "Never mind."[45]

Here is a joke which expresses a political position about Cuba, using a recent controversial incident as the vehicle for its humor:

> Fidel asks for volunteers to form a brigade to rescue Elián; everyone signs up.

Nobel prize winner Rigoberta Menchú has become the subject of many Guatemalan jokes, from right to left along the political spectrum. From the right:

Why do they call Rigoberta Menchú a *chile relleno*?
Because she's always between two *franceses*.

In this joke, the word *franceses* refers to both slices of bread and French
solidarity activists accompanying her (as well as perhaps to sexual connotations). And from the left:

> The Guatemalan army is claiming half the Nobel prize money
> because they say that they did all the work.[46]

INTERETHNIC JOKES AND JOKES ACROSS SOCIAL BOUNDARIES

Another type of joke is the interethnic or interracial joke (commonly
called ethnic jokes), and, more generally, jokes which involve the social
boundaries that operate within a society. These jokes poke fun at stereo-
typic features of a particular social or ethnic group—men, women, old
people, children, Italians, Poles, Jews, representatives of certain professions, inhabitants of certain regions or nations, or students at certain
educational institutions.[47] These jokes are told either by members of
one group about members of another or by members of one group about
themselves. Here are several involving men and women:

> Why are women's brains cheaper than men's brains?
> Because women's are used.

> An old man is sitting on a park bench sobbing. A young man walks
> by and asks him what is wrong and he says, "I'm married to a
> beautiful twenty-two-year-old woman."
> So the young man says, "Well, what's wrong with that?"
> To which the old man replies, "I've forgotten where I live."

In the following joke involving men and women, originally told in Italian, the woman has the last laugh:

> A man sees a woman with blonde hair and says to her: "*bionda
> artificiale* [artificial blonde]."
> The woman responds: "*asino naturale* [natural ass]."

Notice that this joke reframes a verbal duel (see below in this chapter for
a discussion of verbal dueling) and uses rhythm and rhyme as well. The
following jokes involve social boundaries of various kinds:

> The doctor calls up his patient and he says, "I have some good news
> and some bad news."

The patient says, "What's the good news?"
The doctor replies, "You have twenty-four hours to live."
"What?" says the patient. "What could be worse news than that?"
The doctor says, "I forgot to call you yesterday."

A man from Texas meets a man from Vermont and tells him, "Texas
  is so big I can drive all day long and I'm still in Texas."
The man from Vermont responds, "I had a car like that once."

Two Longhorns (students at the University of Texas) and an Aggie
  (a student at Texas A&M University) are planning a hike through
  the desert. Each man packs the provisions that he thinks he will
  need. When they assemble, the Aggie is dumbfounded.
"Why did you bring that canteen?" he asks the first Longhorn.
"There's water in it. If I get hot, I can drink it."
"And why did you bring that cooler?" the Aggie asks the second
  Longhorn.
"There are Popsicles in it. If I get hot, I can eat them."
Now both Longhorns are equally surprised by the Aggie's choice.
  They turn to him and ask, "Why did you bring that car door?"
"Well," the Aggie says, "if I get hot, I can roll down the window."

A Pole sees a genie who says to him, "Make a wish."
The man replies, "Make me a wooden bridge from here to the
  United States."
The genie says, "Do you realize how far that is, how much material
  it would take, how hard it would have to be? Do you have any
  other wish?"
The man says, "Make my three sons into doctors."
To which the genie responds, "How long did you say that bridge
  should be?"

Here is a Corsican joke, based on stereotypes contrasting traditional and
modern Corsicans. It was told in French; I translate it into English here,
without the mock Corsican French accent which was part of the original telling.

A Corsican comes along with a fancy sports car. Just at this
  moment there is a shepherd who is crossing with his flock.
So the shepherd says, "Hey stop stop. I am crossing over with my
  flock."

So the Corsican who is in the car goes, "Hey move away from there. Me I have a big car with four hundred horses in it eh. Hurry up hurry up move it on."

So the shepherd lets him pass and the Corsican takes off full speed ahead into the hills. Then several hours later the shepherd as he is climbing back up the road finds the car of the Corsican in a ditch. And the shepherd says to him, "So we are giving water to the horses?"

Many Italian jokes poke fun at *Carabinieri* 'police,' focusing on their presumed stupidity. Here is one:

Two *Carabinieri* want to distinguish their horses from one another. So one goes to the stable and cuts off the ears of one of the horses. Then the other one goes to the stable and cuts off the ears of the other horse. The first of the *Carabinieri*, when he sees that both horses have their ears cut off, cuts off one of the horses' tails. The second *Carabinieri* goes to the stable and does the same. The next day the two *Carabinieri* go to their superior and report that they cannot distinguish their horses because they are both missing ears and tails. The superior responds, "But it's easy, one horse is black and the other one is white."

One type of joke across social boundaries pokes fun at stigmatized individuals in the society—persons with physical or mental infirmities or such behavioral traits as stuttering. In jokes about stutterers and others with speech defects, like jokes about members of particular ethnic groups, tellers dramatize their performances by imitating and taking on stereotypical voices of the characters in the joke. Here is a stuttering joke:

This guy walks into a bar and says, "One sco scotch and s s soda p p please."

The bartender replies, "One sco scotch and s s soda, c c comin' up."

The customer, angry, says to the bartender, "You you you're m m makin' f f fun of m m me."

The bartender replies, "N n n no. I stu stutter t t too."

Then another guy walks in and says to the bartender, "Gimme a Bloody Mary."

To which the bartender replies, "One Bloody Mary, be ready in a second."

Now the original customer is really angry. He says to the bartender,
"S s see. I t t t told you you we were m m m makin' f fun of me."
To which the bartender replies, "N n n n no. I w was m makin' fu
fun of him."

Jokes about social boundaries and ethnic and social relations, like political jokes, have been interpreted both as reinforcing the existing social order, by allowing for a nonserious release of frustration, and as sub-
verting the social order, attacking this order by means of the joke's
content or the particular contexts in which it is performed.[48] These jokes
are funny because they reflect aspects of social structure and culture
which seem or are symbolically portrayed as incongruous, illogical, or
contradictory—for example, Jews all want to assimilate/Jews stick to
themselves; Jews are miserly/Jews show off their wealth ostentatiously,
etc. They tap into social, cultural, racial, and gender relations, and touch
sensitive nerves. They reflect, add to, comment on, challenge, and critique sociocultural structures, patterns, and themes.

There is a fine line between jokes one group tells about another—
whites about blacks, Gentiles about Jews, northern and western Europeans about Italians and Poles, the French about Corsicans, Trinidadians
about people from Barbados, and men about women—and jokes that a
group tells about itself. In the former case, the jokes can be interpreted
as xenophobic, racist, anti-Semitic, or misogynist; in the latter case, as
self-deprecatory or self-mocking. This is particularly the case for subordinate groups and languages—including Native American, African
American, Hispanic American, Jewish/Yiddish, Balinese, Corsican, Ca-
ribbean/creole, and regional Italian, among many others. The interpretation of jokes as racist, xenophobic, hegemonic, and of course, funny
depends on a complex interaction of form, content, context, and intention. For this reason, jokes play an important role in the imagination,
construction, and invention of selves and communities and in the political economy and ideology of language use.[49]

DIRTY JOKES

A most interesting type of joke is the dirty or obscene joke. While a dirty
joke might contain scatological or otherwise obscene vocabulary, its primary characteristic is that the punch line presupposes and actualizes
knowledge considered taboo by the society, usually having to do with
sexual matters. In addition, the dirty joke is an interactional test about
one's knowledge of sex.[50]

A guy is walking down the street and he passes in front of what looks like a nunnery, with a nun sitting outside and a sign that says "Sisters of Charity Bordello: $25 a Time." He asks the nun, "Is it really true?" She says, "Yes," and he says, "OK," and gives $25 and she says, "First door on the right." He goes down there and opens the door. There is a sign on the wall that says "You Have Just Been Screwed by the Sisters of Charity."

A man goes into a store and asks for a box of condoms.
The owner says, "That will be five dollars and tax." The customer says, "Why the tacks? I thought you rolled them on."

What's the bird of peace? The dove.
What's the bird of war? The hawk.
What's the bird of birth control? The swallow.

The following joke only appears to be about sex, but one of the characters in it, and probably the joke recipient as well, is fooled into thinking that it really is:

A woman enters a doctor's office and say, "Say Doctor, what was wrong with that nun who just came running out of your office? She looked terrible."
"Well you know, I examined her and I told her she was pregnant."
"Is she?"
"No, but I sure as hell cured her hiccups."

I conclude with a playful metalinguistic joke which pokes fun of children's (lack of) knowledge about sex and presumably jokes dealing with sex. As in the previous joke and many others also, the person to whom the joke is being told is victimized by being surprised by the punch line.

Two kindergarten girls are talking, and the first says, "Guess what I saw yesterday? A condom on the patio!"
The second responds, "What's a patio?"

JEWISH JOKES

It is worth singling out Jewish jokes because of a long European/American tradition—from Sigmund Freud to Groucho Marx to Mel Brooks to Woody Allen to Jerry Seinfeld—of humor theory and practice, joke telling and joke analysis, based on Jewish humor. What characterizes these jokes as uniquely Jewish, in addition to their representing and expressing the voices and the weapons of the weak, is a certain mischievous self-deprecation combined with a weird, almost surrealistic, yet perhaps talmudic logic. The Jewish worldview is based on a consciousness of centuries of oppression and dialectic with various oppressors, and has come to be expressed in modes of speaking, especially in the Yiddish language. All of this is present in Jewish jokes, which reflect despair and suffering, self-mocking, self-criticism, and self-analysis. In addition, as in all ethnic jokes, certain elements of Jewish life are found in Jewish jokes. These elements include the use of the Yiddish language (or Yiddish English or a mocking Jewish intonation) to tell the jokes the punch lines, classic Jewish characters or personalities felt to belong to Jews (Schnorrer, Schlimazel, Schlemiel, etc.), kosher food, certain holidays, certain clothing, names (e.g., Goldberg, Greenberg, Cohen, Schwartz), the existence of factions or denominations within the Jewish religion, and the ever present anti-Semitic stereotypes and prejudices (especially those accusing Jews of being miserly and always caring about money).[51]

I begin with a riddle joke from the Talmud that expresses the humorous logic so characteristic of Jewish jokes:

Why was man created on the last day?
So that, if pride were to overtake him, one would be able to say to him, "In the creation the mosquito preceded you."[52]

Here are two jokes whose humor derives from a similarly weird logic:

A person has two eggs and asks his friend how he wants them done. The friend says, "One fried and one poached." So he brings his friend the eggs and his friend says, "You fried the wrong one."

There was a gallery owner who had a very good customer. Whenever he had something he thought the customer would like he called him up. So one day he called him up and he said, "I've got just the painting for you. I'm sure you'll like it. Come down and look at it."
So the customer came down and he found a big white canvas with a little black square in the lower right-hand corner. He looked at it and looked at it and said, "I'll take it, I'll buy it." And he bought it.
A week later the same client gets a call from the same gallery owner. He said, "I've got the mate to that picture. You must come down and see it."

So he came down and there was this big white canvas and in the
lower right-hand corner there were two little black squares. And
he looked at it and looked at it and said, "No, I don't think so, I
don't think I like it."
The owner said, "Why not? It's similar to the other one and you
liked that one so much."
The customer said, "Well," he said, "it's too *ungepachket* (fussy)."[53]

Here are several jokes which are self-mocking, focusing on stereotypical
aspects of Jewish personality and social behavior (including a desire to
assimilate):

Mrs. Goldberg, Mrs. Greenberg, and Mrs. Silverberg are talking.
Mrs. Goldberg says, "My son is a lawyer; he takes cases to the
Supreme Court." Mrs. Greenberg says, "My son is a doctor; he
does triple-bypass operations." Mrs. Silverberg says, "I don't have
a son." So the other two women say to her, "So what do you do
for aggravation?"

One day some people, sailing in distant waters, come across a
deserted island and to their surprise find a Jewish man living
there alone. He explains that he is the sole survivor of a ship-
wreck. He says that he survives by fishing and gathering edible
plants, and then takes the visitors to one end of the island where
he has constructed a large synagogue. He says, "This is where I
pray." They are quite impressed. Then he takes them to the other
end of the island where he has constructed another synagogue.
"What is that one for?" the visitors ask. "That's the one I don't
go to," he replies.

Two men, they're partners and they did very well in their business
and they decided it was time to fix up the store and they bought
a new building and they made a new office and they hired a beautiful young receptionist and then they thought, "Well gee Goldberg and Stein doesn't sound fancy enough for such a fancy operation. Let's think of a good fancy name."
So they thought and they thought and they came up with Braddock
and Braddock. They thought that sounded elegant. So the company became Braddock and Braddock.
And one day a customer came in and said to the receptionist, "I'd
like to talk to Mr. Braddock."
And she said, "Which one do you want, Goldberg or Stein?"

Here are several jokes about money and finances, beginning with one that hinges on an important element of Jewish dress:

This is a story about a man who was a gambler and he went to the races every day and he lost a lot of money and one night he had a dream. An angel came to him in the dream and said, "If you will bet on a horse that has the name of a hat, you'll win."

So he went back to the racetrack the next day and he looked down the list of names and he found Top Hat. So he bet on Top Hat and he won. The next day he bet on Straw Hat and he won. And the next day he bet on Fedora and he won.

But the following day when he came to the racetrack and he looked down the list of names, he couldn't find anything that reminded him of a hat. So he picked a horse at random, put all his money on it, and lost, big.

On the way home he met a friend and he said to him, "How did you do at the racetrack today?"

So he told him the story about the angel and the dream and so on.

So his friend said to him, "Who won that race?"

"Oh," he said, "Some dodo called Yarmulke."

Two Jewish men are losing their shirts on the stock market. One of them, Cohen, says to his friend Greenberg, "I can't sleep."

To which his friend Greenberg replies, "I have no trouble. I sleep like a baby."

"How do you do it?" Cohen says.

Greenberg replies, "I get up every two hours and cry."

Two retired businessmen met on the beach in Miami. And one said to the other, "What did you do before you retired?"

He said, "Oh, I had a ladies' blouse factory. And one day there was a terrible fire and it burned down the factory and all the contents of the factory. So I decided when I got the money from the insurance company I wouldn't rebuild. I'll go down to Miami and live the rest of my life in peace."

"So," he said, "What did you do before you retired?"

He said, "Oh, I had a men's pants factory. There was a terrible flood and it destroyed the factory and all the merchandise in it and I too decided when I got the money from the insurance company that I wouldn't rebuild. I'd go down to Miami and live the good life."

So the other man thought for a while and said to him, "So tell me, how do you start a flood?"

A man dies and they were having a wake and a lot of his friends came to the wake. And four of them came up to the casket and they looked down at him and one of them said, "Gee, Sam, I feel so bad, you lent me twenty-five dollars a long time ago and I never gave it back to you." And he took out twenty-five dollars and he put it in the coffin.
The second one did the same and the third one also.
And the fourth one looked at the seventy-five dollars in the coffin. And he was a real shrewdy. And he said, "You know Sam, you lent me twenty-five dollars too. But I don't have any cash." So he wrote out a check for a hundred dollars and he took seventy-five dollars change.

Notice how several of these jokes, especially the ones having to do with money, could easily be intended and/or interpreted as anti-Semitic if told by non-Jews. Yet when told by Jews, as is the case with the jokes reported here, they are intended and interpreted as mocking the anti-Semitic stereotype. Here are two jokes about relations with other groups:

The priest and the rabbi were sitting next to each other at the Bnai Brith dinner and after a while the priest said, "I know that you're orthodox so you're not supposed to eat pork. Have you ever tasted it?"
The rabbi says, "Well, yes I have, a couple of times. And I know you're supposed to be celibate. Have you ever . . . ?"
The priest says, "Well, actually yes, a couple of times."
The rabbi says, "Better than pork isn't it?"

This is a story about a man who went into a restaurant and he was waited on by a Chinese waiter. It was a Jewish restaurant and the Chinaman spoke perfect Yiddish. So when he [the Chinaman] went back into the kitchen he [the customer] called the owner over and said, "How come this Chinaman speaks such perfect Yiddish?"
"Oh," he [the owner] says, "Don't let him hear you. He thinks we're teaching him English."

And finally, here are three jokes which mock Jews' most significant other, Gentiles, by subtly and covertly contrasting Gentile behavior with stereotypes that Gentiles, as well as Jews, have about Jews.[54]

A Gentile walks into a clothing store, looks at a jacket, and asks, "How much does it cost?" The salesman replies, "Five hundred dollars," and the Gentile says, "OK, I'll take it."

Two Gentile businessmen meet on a street. One asks the other, "How's business?" and the other says, "Great!"

A Gentile calls his mother on the phone and says, "Mom, I know I was going to eat with you tonight, but I just don't have time." She answers, "Don't worry about it."

METAJOKES

As a final joke category, there are jokes which in one way or another comment on other jokes and joke structure. Children are fond of this type of joke, but adults tell them as well. Here is one which starts off like a narrative joke about men in a bar—a quite common theme with a quite common opening line. But the pun which reframes the joke tricks the recipient, who never gets to hear the expected narrative following the familiar opening:

Two guys walk into a bar and the third one ducks.

Here is a wonderfully illustrative metajoke that has embedded within it, in a most condensed and reduced form, three other jokes. It offers discourse analysts an important message concerning the relationship between text and context, or performance, focusing on the significance of appropriate telling.

A new prisoner in a jail is sitting around with fellow inmates and they begin to tell jokes. One of them yells out "Number one," and everyone cracks up with laughter. Another yells out "Number five," and again everyone laughs heartily. The new prisoner asks, "Why is everyone laughing? You are just calling out numbers." To which one of the inmates responds, "We've been here so long that we don't need to hear the full joke. Just hearing the number reminds us of the joke and cracks us up." The next time the prisoners start telling jokes, again one yells out, "Number one," and once again they all crack up. And again one yells out, "Number five," and they all laugh. So the new prisoner figures he'll tell one too. He yells out, "Number nine." But no one laughs; he is met by stony silence. He asks the others, "What

happened? I thought all you had to do was call out a number."
To which they respond, "Some people know how to tell a joke
and some people don't."

JOKE TELLINGS AND PERFORMANCES

As the previous joke illustrates so well, there are interesting relationships between the form, structure, and content of jokes; the ways in
which they are told and performed and used interactionally; and the
ways in which they reflect and express social, cultural, and ideological
concerns. Jokes are often conventionally framed, opening with expressions such as "Did you hear the one about?" or "Here's a silly joke my
brother told me" and closing with one of another set of similar expressions. And jokes can occur in rounds, organized by form or topic, or both.
Like other verbal forms that occur in conversational contexts, jokes can
be viewed as social-interactional achievements. Because they involve relating unstated assumptions to the stated punch line, they are tests and
displays of intelligence and knowledge—for both tellers and listener-
recipients, or the audience. Tellers must perform jokes in such a way
that they demonstrate understanding of them. Listeners must "get" a
joke and either laugh or make some other conventional response, such
as a groan, at the appropriate moment. Listeners often begin to respond
before the punch line, both showing that and checking whether they get
the point before the joke is completed. This is especially the case in
jokes that deal with relatively taboo topics such as sex.[55] Here is a joke
told on the radio by broadcaster A to broadcaster B. Notice the location
and form of B's interjected responses within the quite common tripartite
narrative-joke structure.

A: A new parish priest looks exactly like Frank Sinatra. His first
day on the job he begins making rounds to visit people. The first
door he knocks on is opened by an old woman who exclaims,
"Frank Sinatra, Frank Sinatra," to which the priest responds,
"No, no, I'm just the new parish priest. I've come to visit you."
Then he knocks on a second door and an elderly couple opens
it, exclaiming in unison, "Frank Sinatra, Frank Sinatra." Again
the priest responds, "No, no, I'm just the new parish priest. I've
come to visit you." Then he knocks on a third door, and when
the door opens there stands a beautiful blonde with a see-through
negligee.
B: I knew this was coming.

A: When the woman sees the priest she says, "Frank Sinatra, Frank Sinatra." And the priest responds, "Doo bee doo bee doo."

B: Oooo.

In North American speech communities, in English, the groan is the conventional way of showing for both puns and jokes that a recipient-listener has understood the point or source of humor and that, at the same time, he or she is intellectually or socially superior to it.

There is, no doubt, pleasure to be had in the display of wit. Joke performances are an occasion for individuals to put on a little act and to show off. They verbally and publicly display their knowledge of various subjects and their ability to represent voices, imitate dialogues, and stereotype actions. It is also through person-to-person joke telling that jokes circulate quickly and widely—in addition, more recently, to email and the internet, in which joke-telling performances are framed electronically.

Jokes are enjoyable and pleasurable to both tellers and listeners. They are a form of verbal relaxation, time off and time out from the more real, literal, serious, and informational uses of language. But jokes also have an aggressive component, noted by Freud, who studied them together with puns under the rubric *witz* 'wit.' This aggression is both social and personal. And there are two types of victims, which were not sufficiently distinguished by Freud and his followers. First is the victim in the text of the joke itself—the Jew, Pole, Italian, woman, Californian, or stutterer who is being mocked. Second, there are the listeners, who are suddenly given short intelligence tests and, whether or not they want to, forced to publicly display their knowledge or lack of knowledge about a particular, perhaps taboo, area. In actual tellings, these two kinds of victims can be combined in various ways. For example, non-Jews can tell jokes about Jews and vice versa. Since jokes, like puns, can be used to obtain and hold the floor, they involve interactional as well as personal aggression.

Puns and jokes, like all speech play more generally, should not be viewed as marginal or insignificant communicative behavior. These seemingly small and unimportant forms involve a condensation of basic processes and principles of discourse—such as cohesion, disjunction, frame construction and breaking, and the relationship between the said and the unsaid—as well as the psychological, interactional, and socio-cultural underpinnings of discourse. The joke about Governor Wallace illustrates extreme condensation in the relationship between the said and the unsaid, and thus shows the extreme laconicity of jokes.

I end this section on jokes—quite appropriately, I think, given the subject of the book—with three jokes about language that provide different views and contrasting ideologies about the importance of linguistic diversity.

A Swiss guy, looking for directions, pulls up at a bus stop where two Englishmen are waiting. "Entschuldigung, können Sie deutsch sprechen?" he says. The two Englishmen just stare at him.
"Excusez-moi, parlez-vous français?" The two continue to stare.
"Parlate italiano?" No response. "¿Hablan ustedes español?" Still nothing. The Swiss guy drives off, extremely disgusted.
The first Englishman turns to the second and says, "You know, maybe we should learn a foreign language."
"Why?" says the other. "That bloke knew four languages, and it didn't do him any good."

People who speak three languages are trilingual. Those who speak two, bilingual. What do you call those who speak one? Americans.

A momma cat and six little kittens were walking along the street and they encountered a ferocious dog who barked viciously at them. And the little kittens wanted to run away. And the momma cat said, "Oh no, you watch me." And she walked up to the dog and she barked right back at him. And the dog was so taken aback to hear a cat bark that he moved away and let them pass. And then when she got to the corner of the street she gathered her little kittens and said, "You see, children, how important it is to know a second language."[56]

Put-ons, Trickster Behavior, and Trickster Tales

In put-ons, an addressee in a conversational interchange or an audience is tricked into believing that something is the case that in actuality is not the case. In terms of frame analysis, the victim is led to believe in one frame of reference while another is actually in effect.[57] Put-ons can no doubt occur in all societies. But in some they are conventional and recognized as such. Throughout Native America there exists a form of put-on in which one individual dupes another with a very brief, indeed fleeting statement. For example, Apaches victimize other Apaches for a moment by offering a verbal portrait of the other as a white man.[58] The Kuna tell elaborate personal narratives which seem quite serious but are actually humorous put-ons concerning serious topics such as starvation, sickness, or death. These narratives are used to trick both other Kuna and outsiders. They are very funny joking interactions, and yet somehow deeply serious as well.[59]

These passing and fleeting trickster behaviors are related to traditional trickster narratives or tales. Actual cases of trickster behavior can become the basis for elaborated narratives. And traditional, conventional trickster narratives are constructed out of individual instances of put-ons, moments of trickster behavior. Beloved in Native America, these narratives are a centerpiece of Native American literature. But they are found the world over and spread very easily; in fact, many Native American trickster tales may very well have originated in Europe or Africa. In their Native American context, they are remarkably adapted, in terms of ecology, culture, society, and performance practices. A favorite North American trickster is Coyote.[60]

One popular Kuna trickster story is "The Agouti Story," about a rivalry/competition between Jaguar and Agouti, a Central American long-legged rodent and the Kuna equivalent of the North American Coyote. This story, like other Kuna humorous stories, is told by chiefs or other political leaders in the evenings, before public meetings in the central village gathering house, or in the daytime, on the occasion of the visit of dignitaries from other villages or on days on when, for various reasons, people do not go to work in the nearby jungle. The teller, Chief Muristo Pérez, is a great storyteller. He combines suspense and humor as he tells the story to his spokesman Armando, in front of an audience who loves every bit of it in spite of having heard it performed many times before. He modulates his voice, alternating fast and slow and loud and soft speech, and including rhetorical pauses. He varies his pitch pattern to represent the voices of the animal characters. Like Coyote and other animal characters in North American trickster stories, who are involved in quite similar, sometimes identical episodes, the animals in the Agouti story are humanlike in their foibles and their conversational joking and trickery. They are models of and models for Kuna human behavior, and human behavior more generally.[61]

In this representation of the story, in order to render the oral features and rhythm of the actual performance I use the following conventions. Lines are determined by a combination of falling pitch and long pause. Long pauses without accompanying falling pitch are represented by a large space between words. Extra loud speech is indicated by means of capital letters. Dashes between syllables indicate stretched-out speech. Expressive lengthening of sounds is indicated by the doubling of letters. Faster speech is indicated by a dotted underline under the words that are spoken faster. When part of a line is higher in pitch, this is indicated by raising the words. When a whole line is higher in pitch, this is indicated by ^ placed before the line.

Well listen Armando.
So let's listen to a bit of a story now.
A story.
It's "The Agouti Story."
So   and Agouti   Jaguar the two of them   they were
    about to compete with each other.
And Jaguar   Agouti the two of them Agouti   Agouti is a
    trickster ah.
Jaguar is a hunter.
He got there and saw him ah.
So Agouti is sit-ting-up-straight.
Uncle saw him Jaguar did.
He started chasing him.
When he started chasing him   over there say, it's true it is said.
So Agouti is sitting eating.
So "I'm sitting eating *ikwa* fruit" he says.
On top of a hill   seated.
Sitting on top of a hill, sitting eating, there to
Uncle   Agouti says to Uncle.
"Now you are going to eat too" he says it is said.
"He is going along chasing him ah, he is going to eat" he says
    "he is going to eat his head."
(Armando interjects: it's true his head is going to be caught I think.)
"In point of fact" he says, "what are you sitting eating it's true I am
    going to eat some too" he says.
It's true it is said.
"How did you split it open ah?" he said.
^"How were you able to split it open?"
"In point of fact" he says "I split it open with my balls" see it is
    said.
^"With my balls I split it open.
You watch" he says ah.
He got a rock a rock a rock   he got.
Agouti ooopened up his balls his balls he op he set them
    against the side of the hill.
TAK the *ikwa* fruit TAK AK.
(Armando interjects: Wow what pain!)
"You see" it is said ah.
It's true it is said.
Ah Jaguar is astounded ah.

"Here you're going to do it like that too" he said to him.
Well he got a rock for him too.
But the other one placed the *ikwa* fruit right on top of his balls ah.
Did you hear?
This Agouti he tricked him for the fun of it.
This one he smashed against the stone the stone he didn't do it on
   his balls.
But Jaguar is going to place it right on his balls.
Then he diiid it   TAK.
So he smashed him in the banana.
(Audience laughs uproariously.)
It's true it is said.
Well   so   he diiid it he finished off his balls it is said.
That big boy Agouti knocked him out he-sure-made-him-jump-a-
   round.
Ah.
Poor Jaguar.
He passed out   he fainted.
And Agouti took off again started running again.
Running running running run laugh-ing a-long down the path ah.⁶²

Proverbs

Proverbs and riddles belong to a group of related speech-play forms
which include aphorisms, maxims, and other wise sayings. They are
characterized by the use of metaphorical or figurative meanings which
encapsulate basic philosophical truths about life, and by clearly recognizable linguistic structures. They are used and heard in everyday
speech, as well as on more formal occasions. They are associated with
traditional knowledge and older generations, but at the same time they
are laughed at and made fun of and can be a great source of humor.

Proverbs are short and concise. They have a binary structure in which
one two-part relationship is compared or related to another. Well-known
examples in English include

Better late than never.
Birds of a feather flock together.
When it rains it pours.
A stitch in time saves nine.
A rolling stone gathers no moss.
A bird in the hand is worth two in the bush.

From other languages:

FRENCH

Faute de grives on mange des merles.
'Since we don't have thrushes we eat blackbirds [less appreciated gastronomically].'
L'union fait la force.
'In union there is strength.'
Qui fait de soi fait pour trois.
'He who does it for himself does it for three.'

Notice that the last two proverbs actually contradict one another, a not uncommon phenomenon in proverb usage.

ITALIAN

Due cuori una cabana.
'Two hearts one hearth.'
Il grosso pesce mangia sempre il piccolo.
'The big fish always eats the little one.'
Tanto la gatta va al lardo finche ci lascia lo zompino.
'Every time the cat goes to the lard [to steal], she leaves a trace.'
  (= As long as one goes to steal, one leaves a trace.)

SPANISH

Si hay más perros hay más pulgas.
'If there are more dogs there are more fleas.'
Dime con quien andas y te diré quien eres.
'Tell me who you go about with and I will tell you who you are.'
Mientras menos burros más elotes.
'The fewer the donkeys, the more corn cobs there are.'
Hablando del rey de Roma y el que la cabeza asoma.
'Speaking of the king, and suddenly his head appears. (= Speaking of the devil.)

TOBAGO (CREOLE)

One eye dog na rampa a san.
'A dog with one eye wouldn't play in the sand.' (= Don't try to do more than you are capable of.)
What sweet in goat mout sour in di bam bam.
'What is sweet in the goat's mouth is sour in the ass.' (= What you enjoy now will get you in trouble later.)

Proverbs from non-Western languages and cultures might be difficult for the uninformed reader to interpret out of context, and yet they have the usual proverb form and structure:

FROM CHAMULA (A MAYAN LANGUAGE OF CHIAPAS, MEXICO)
The road is still open, but it will close.[63]

Proverbs often include words or phrases which are felt to be poetic or archaic, and which have such features as notable rhythm, rhyme, alliteration, assonance, and parallelism. One aspect of their poetic brevity is the elimination of words or phrases found in everyday speech, such as the verb *to be*. Proverbs are figurative and indexical, metaphorically relating one realm to another—typically a concrete, specific event to a more general, universalistic message or truth. Thus a nurse in a hospital, helping a woman who has been bedridden to slowly begin walking again, says, "Rome was not built in a day." And a man, upon entering a men's room and beginning to urinate in a urinal beside another man who is also urinating, says, "When in Rome."[64]

Part of the meaning of proverbs, then, is an implied or potential rhetorical usage which may or may not be actualized in use. Proverbs are often overtly framed in ways which provide either evidence of their place in tradition or distance from their utterer or both. Thus "Like my Mom says," "As my grandmother used to say," "You know what they say in my business," "As the French say," or even just "Well."

Proverbs occur in different types of contexts. In social interactions, they can be used to answer a question, give advice, or sum things up—ending a topic or an entire conversation, or moving metaphorically from a specific topic to a general point. The French proverb presented above, *Faute de grives on mange des merles* 'Since we don't have thrushes we eat blackbirds,' was used by a cardplayer who, when playing with only one other person, was asked if it would not be better to play with three other people instead of one. The proverb which he used as a response then means 'We make do with what we have.' The Spanish proverb *Si hay más perros hay más pulgas* 'If there are more dogs there are more fleas' was uttered by a musician in a band to sum up his discussion of what happens when you enlarge the size of your band.[65] *Mientras menos burros más elotes* 'The fewer the donkeys, the more corn cobs there are' was uttered by one of two people eating peanuts when a third one said she did not want any. The proverb was used to mean 'We get more that way.'[66]

Proverbs can be attention getters or devices used to get the floor in a conversation. In this sense, proverbs, like other metaphorical expressions, are part of the strategic operation of conversation. This strategy can be both social interactional and economic, as when a proverb such as this Moroccan one is used during a bargaining exchange in a market: "You're trying to buy a camel for the price of a donkey."[67]

Notice that proverbs are simultaneously indexical in two senses. Their figurative language indexes a general cultural belief in the society in which they are used. At the same time, their usage indexes a particular and specific social-interactional strategy. They relate areas familiar to speakers, like body parts or aspects of ecology, to activities of the immediate moment, from cardplaying to politics.

Proverbs are a reflection of cultural values wherever they are found, and are often felt to be traditional, wise statements of truth. In the Texas state legislature, legislators sometimes use folksy proverbs in their political speeches in order to be seen as more rural and traditional—and also to be purposely funny—even if they are actually urban attorneys. These proverbs often describe elements of Texas ecology and rural practices such as agriculture.

> Every bell you hear ain't the dinner bell.
> The skunk can't tell the buzzard he stinks.
> Don't go throwing manure uphill, or it's liable to roll back in your face.
> More cotton will grow in a crooked row than a straight one.[68]

Similarly, here is a Texas lawyer in a phone conversation after a public meeting, talking about real-estate developers:

> You know what they say in my business: Pigs get fat and hogs get slaughtered.[69]

Here is a student at the University of Texas arguing at a university-wide faculty meeting for more support for students:

> From the students' perspective, we can't sell the farm if we don't have someplace to live.[70]

Among the Mayan Chamula and probably other Native Mesoamerican groups, proverbs are so deeply embedded in ordinary, everyday speech that they are sometimes difficult to notice, even though they have a generally constant form, use puns, and are both humorous and metaphorical. Purposely ambiguous linguistically and socially, they are used to subtly chastise people for deviations from appropriate social behavior.[71] In Bali, proverblike aphorisms are part of the banter and verbal dueling of which the Balinese are forever fond, both in everyday speech as well as more ritual- and public-dance dramas and shadow-puppet plays.[72]

Proverbs themselves can become the object of play. Various forms of manipulation are possible. Proverbs can be abbreviated: "When in Rome," "A bird in the hand."[73] They can be altered in some way, sometimes to the point of absurdity: "You reap what you sow and all that"; "You can teach a pit bull to squat, but that won't get you enough eggs for an omelet." The frame can be elaborated in conjunction with an abbreviation: "You know what they say about a bird in the hand"; "We need it, it'd be a bird in the hand"; "Brevity soul of wit Shakespeare." They can be turned on their heads in terms of their expressed rhetorical function: "Oh well, never do today what you can put off until tomorrow"; "Flattery will get you everywhere." Interestingly, since proverbs are meant to be taken metaphorically and not literally, their literal use is quite humorous: "Don't cry over spilt milk," uttered to someone who was upset because she had just spilled milk on the table. Proverbs can be mingled: "A bird in the bush gathers no moss"; "You can't vote against the hand that feeds you all the time or you won't get fat." They can be changed so that the second part is not proverbial, thus rendering the entire utterance a joke: "He who lives in glass houses should dress in the basement"; "Hell hath no fury like a CEO on a spiritual mission." A bit of obscenity, always a potential in speech play, can be added: "Two many cooks fuck up the cookies." A humorous proverb can be based on an actual one but manipulated for humor, again resulting in a kind of joke. Thus the following proverb is derived from "When you smile the world smiles with you; when you frown you frown alone" (again with a bit of obscenity): "When you snore you sleep alone; when you fart you stand alone." A proverb can be invented, using the usual proverbial structural pattern, as when the chair of a meeting announces a break by saying, "The mind absorbs no more than the seat endures." Finally, manipulated, playful proverbs can cut across an interaction, constituting a clever comeback, a miniature verbal duel, as in the following exchange in which two women are talking about dating:

A: Well, you can lead a horse to water.
B: Yeah, but you can't get it to ask you out.

Proverbs, quite like riddles (see below), can become the focus of verbal duels that refer to no topic other than the proverbs themselves:

A: A fool and his money are soon parted.
B: Yeah, but lack of money is the root of all evil.

A: Curiosity killed the cat.

B: And satisfaction brought it back.

Riddles

Like proverbs, riddles are metaphorical, and relate contrasting classifications and conceptual frameworks. They occur in a question-and-answer format in which the question is enigmatic and challenges the answerer to figure it out. The question is mystifying, misleading, or puzzling, posed as a problem to be solved or guessed, something difficult to understand. The answer is surprising but clever. At the same time, a riddle is a kind of definition or description whose referent must be guessed. Here is an example from English:

Question: Twenty-four horses set upon a bridge.

Answer: Teeth on gums.[74]

As with proverbs, readers unfamiliar with a language, and especially a culture, will probably not understand its riddles.[75] Also, the question part of many riddles is like the first part of a proverb. And, like proverbs, riddles contain implicit rhetorical messages. In the United States, riddles are often used by and associated with children and are used as jokes. Here is a classic one, which depends on a pun:

Question: What's black and white and read all over?

Answer: A newspaper.

Children also manipulate these riddle jokes, to add to the play, as in another classic in which a literal answer is expected and the person providing the answer is duped if he or she looks for a figurative one:

Question: Why did the chicken cross the road?

Answer: To get to the other side.

Riddle jokes, like knock-knock jokes—which, as noted above, are also part of children's speech-play culture—may also be developmentally significant, an aspect of children's acquisition of adult speech-play forms and competence in discourse more generally. But adults also tell riddlelike jokes. Here is one told during the period of the Olympic games:

Question: What's the hardest thing about skating?

Answer: The ice.[76]

Adult riddlelike jokes often take the form of a humorous attack on a particular social group, as in light-bulb jokes:

> Question: How many Californians does it take to screw in a light bulb?
> Answer: Four. One to screw in the bulb and three to share the experience.

In other societies riddles are used by adults as well as children. The Kuna create riddles out of *play names:* short, humorous labels for various objects, usually animals, and that are based on physical characteristics. Examples are *sortukkin nakue* 'hangs by the tail' (= a monkey) and *naras asu* 'orange nose' (= a curassow [large Central American and South American bird]). Play names are used in a riddling game, in which one individual mentions a play name and challenges a partner to name the animal.

> Question: *pete kapur ipya kwat* 'Hey you, the one with hot-pepper eyes?'
> Answer: *suka* 'crab.'[77]

Riddles are a speech-play component of the African diaspora. They are found, for example, in the West Indies, where they often refer to power relationships and situations, including those of father and child, black and white, man and animal, and life and death. Here are some examples from St. Vincent, told in the context of an all-night wake:

> Question: My father have a cock and every time it crow, it crow fire.
> Answer: A gun.
> Question: My father build a house with one post and many sill.
> Answer: Umbrella.[78]

The Afro-Brazilian *jongo* is a riddle-based song genre in which both the riddle and its solution are improvised:

RIDDLE

Debaixo de papai velho	Under old father,
Menino tá sepurtado.	Boy is buried.
Quero contar no meu ponto:	I want to tell you in my verse:
Menino foi interrado.	Boy was interred.

ANSWER

Meu irmão, sendo mais velho,	My brother, being older,
Licença peço pr'ocê:	I ask you to excuse me.

Vou desinterrar o menino	I'll now exhume the boy
Pra nós tudo aqui beber.	So all of us here can drink.

Both the riddle and its answer/solution are metaphorical. The "old father" represents the *tambu,* the largest drum used in the *jongo;* the "boy" represents a bottle of cane spirits. The singer has hidden his drink under the instrument.[79]

In Bali, there are many metaphoric, riddling bantering routines. One of these involves playful *sesonggan* 'aphorisms,' such as

damar di abing (literally 'lamp in a steep embankment')

with its alliteration and sound symbolism, the reply to which is the reduplicated

kunang-kunang 'lightning bug'

all of which metaphorically means 'Do you have a girl friend?' (*tunangan*), because *tunangan* sounds like *kunang-kunang.* In this complex verbal performance, one utterance means/suggests another which in turns means/suggests another in a network of metaphorical and punful play. Another humorous *sesonggan* is:

Question: *mekunyit di alas* 'turmeric in the forest'
Answer: *ketemu* 'spice'

Ketemu, which is a type of spice, also means 'acquaintance' and, in this context, 'boyfriend/girlfriend' or 'lover'. Still another of many:

Ketut meatin kayu 'Ketut is the heart of a tree,' which means
   'Ketut is sleeping.'

The complicated verbal play involved here is that the coarse-level Balinese word *pules* 'sleep,' when pronounced quickly, is *les,* which also means the inner wood (i.e., heart) of a tree.[80]

Verbal Dueling

Verbal dueling is the competitive use of language within a gamelike structure, with rules that are known and used by participants. In a sense verbal dueling is a formalization or ritualization of the banter that frequently emerges in everyday joking behavior. The basic principle of verbal dueling is that the witty banter is focused into a dialogic ritual between two participants. Each must top the utterance of the other with a comeback which is recognized to be better. Rhyme and rhythm as well as phonological, syntactic, and semantic play are involved. In some traditions, verbal dueling combines with musical dueling. Highly evaluated comebacks bring about maximum semantic shifts with minimal change of form. Verbal dueling is widespread in the world. It has been studied in the Mediterranean region; among Native Americans, European Americans, and African Americans; and in Oceania.[81] It tends to involve obscenities, often couched in allusive language. And it seems to be practiced by men, especially adolescent men, more than by women— though it is not limited to men. Here are some particularly characteristic examples of dueling sequences recorded among African Americans in New York City:

> A: Your momma's a peanut man!
> B: Your momma's a ice-man!
> C: Your momma's a fire man!

> A: Your momma's a truck driver!
> B: Your father sell crackerjacks!
> C: Your mother look like a crackerjack!

> A. Your mother got on sneakers!
> B. Your mother wear high-heeled sneakers to church!
> C: Your mother wear high-heeled sneakers to come out and play on the basketball court!

> A: I'll take you to the last man.
> B: I'll take your mother.
> C: I took your mother.[82]

As these examples demonstrate, verbal dueling involves a dialogue sequence or chain in which each member of the chain is ranked in terms of the strength of the linguistic forms involved. This linguistic strength can be lexical (run/walk, eat/drink, obscene/non-obscene), grammatical (more complex/less complex), or semantic (especially semantic shifts with minimal change of form, as in took/take). Socially and culturally, verbal dueling focuses on the boundary between the literal and the play, which is essential to the creation of frames in discourse. It tests and protects the boundaries of social relations and taboo topics. And like riddles, to which it is related, verbal dueling is quintessentially interactional and especially dialogic.

Throughout Latin America there exist forms of verbal dueling which are structured musically as well as verbally. They derive from the medieval Iberian minstrel tradition, combined with an African call-and-response interactional pattern and Amerindian elements as well. They include such forms as Spanish American *décimas, coplas,* and *huapangos* and Northeastern Brazilian *desafios,* as well as carnival songs in such places as Panama where a procession from one part of town sings insults aimed at people from another part of town.

All of these forms involve competition in both musical play and verbal wit. They are typically performed by two singers, accompanied by string instruments such as guitars or violas or percussion instruments such as tambourines. The singers alternate singing verses that combine fixed forms with improvised forms. There is a conventional metric and rhyme scheme. The verbal content is comical and satirical, often using double meanings. And it is frequently metacommunicative.[83]

Here are some examples from a vibrant *copla* tradition in the town of La Plata in Southern Colombia. These *coplas* consist of four octosyllabic lines. Performed in the context of a carnival-like festival, they are intended to be humorous and offer social criticism, and, as in the following, often include pornographic verses couched in ambiguous words and phrases with multiple meanings:

Cuando dos se quieren bien,
se quieren como hermanitos.
Ella le lleva la jaula
y él lleva el pajarito.
When a couple are really in love,
they love each other like brother and sister.
She brings the cage for him
and he brings the little bird for her.[84]

In the following *copla* duel, as reflected in the words at the end, two individuals, labeled A1 and A2, are dueling against one, labeled B, who criticizes A1 and A2 for using vulgar language:

A1: *Me ha tratado de grosero*
y yo lo he perdonado
porque afuera de ser mi taita,
otros más mal me han tratado.

He has called me vulgar
and I've forgiven him

for besides his being my father,
I've been treated much worse by others.

B: *Lo que antes comentaba,*
lo dije por estos lares,
porque aquí hay muchos copleros
que se pasan de vulgares.
What I commented earlier,
I've said in this spot before,
for there are a lot of copleros here
who quickly turn very vulgar.

A2: *El Señor Augusto Cuéllar,*
que mi copla ya rechaza
con esos ojos de avispa
y ese jeta 'e cucaracha.
Mr. Augusto Cuéllar,
who rejects my *copla*
with those wasp-like eyes
and that cockroach mouth.

B: *Dicen que el avispa pica*
y eso me decía mi tío
Para pelear con el Cuéllar,
tal vez usted está muy frío.
They say that the wasp can sting
my uncle told me so
to pick a fight with me,
well maybe you're not quite up to it.

Si Augusto sigue jodiendo
tendrá un problema conmigo
yo lo chuzo en la barriga,
yo lo chuzo en el ombligo.
If Augusto keeps bothering me
he'll be in trouble with me
I'll sting him in the belly,
and I'll sting him in his navel.

El Señor Augusto Cuéllar
el se cree la Mamá 'e Dios.
El cuenta que con Nieto
ya nosotros somos dos.

Mr. Augusto Cuéllar
thinks he's God's own mother [a big shot].
He can count that with Nieto
we've got him two against one.[85]

I return now to another part of the world, Bali, where verbal duels are
a basic ingredient of everyday verbal interaction. The Balinese are forever fond of punning and constructing comebacks and verbal duels out
of puns. The puns are often made possible because of the existence of
many words in the various languages or speech levels in use in Bali that
have different meanings but identical or near-identical pronunciation.

A very common playful routine in the streets, food stalls, and stores
of Bali is the punful comeback. Here is a typical routine:

An individual, A, says to another, B, in Indonesian:
sudah siap 'are you ready' (literally 'already ready').
B responds, in Indonesian: *sudah ayam* 'already a chicken.'

This comeback, which does not reply referentially and logically to the
question, is a play on the fact that *siap*, which means 'ready' in Indonesian, means 'chicken' in low or ordinary Balinese, and that *ayam*, in addition to meaning 'chicken' in Indonesian, also means 'chicken' in high
Balinese. The humor of using the Indonesian (and Balinese) word *ayam*
in the comeback depends on the bilingualism of both speakers, and,
probably at a deeper and more serious level, of much of the Balinese
speech community. To continue the dialogue, A responds to B:

sudah bebek 'already a duck'

Bebek is both Indonesian and low Balinese, and of course adds to the paradigmatic to syntagmatic projection of languages and levels that of the
semantic field: fowl.

Such verbal dueling is felt to be quite humorous. It involves a kind of
verbal skidding and is valued as demonstrating linguistic virtuosity. At
the same time it constitutes an exploration of and commentary on the
complex sociolinguistic situation of Bali, drawing on the intersection of
levels of Balinese and the national language, Indonesian. Here is a punful comeback based on mispronunciation with suggestion of meaning:

Two men (A and B) are conversing:
A says: *mepamit* 'excuse me'
B responds: *mamwamit*

This is verbal babble, though *mamwit* means 'to go.' The *m/b* interchange used for humorous purposes here occurs also in a popular mocking greeting in use in the town of Ubud. This greeting is *mintang milem* '[hi] film star,' which is derived from *bintang pilem* 'film star,' in which the word *pilem* is made to sound like Délem, (the humorous shadow-puppet character to whom it is always funny to compare others), or perhaps Malén (Twalén; another humorous character from the shadow-puppet theater). The greeting *mintang milem* is often responded to with *bintang malam* 'night star' (which often means 'prostitute'). Another variation I have heard on this routine is as follows, with A and B:

A: bintang pilem
B: bintang palem (dish of shrimp and coconut)
C: bintang malam

It is no doubt difficult for an outsider to Bali or to other places in the world where strong verbal-dueling traditions exist to imagine that such playful verbal creativity is spontaneous, invented on the spot. And no doubt there are many fixed routines which are so common that many people know them in a memorized or formulaic way. This is true not only of puns and punful comebacks, but also of the many metaphorlike and riddlelike bantering routines so widespread in Bali. At the same time, in addition to formulaic routines, and precisely because comebacks and verbal dueling are such cultural foci, individuals can be creative, spontaneous, and innovative with them. The fact that a particular pun or verbal routine has been used before or is known to others does not mean that its reuse is not creative. Quite the contrary. The pun or routine itself is a resource for further play, further puns and verbal duels, as well as for its use in either expected or unexpected contexts, linguistic and/or sociocultural. Another good example is the rhymed play with place-names, used in response to the question *kija* 'where are you going?' Some standard replies are:

ke Buléleng meli tenggek céléng 'to Buleleng to buy pig's head'
ke Bangli meli tali 'to Bangli to buy cord'

But new ones are also created on the spot, such as:

ke Lombok meli rokok 'to Lombok to buy cigarettes'

And of course today's creation is tomorrow's routine.

Many quite similar examples of puns, comebacks, verbal duels, and riddle-metaphor banter can be found in the humorous moments of Balinese dance dramas and shadow-puppet plays, thus providing continuity between everyday verbal behavior and artistic and ritual performances. Dance dramas and shadow-puppet plays, precisely because they are artistic performances, carry such verbal play and humor even further and take it in various directions. At the same time the play of the everyday provides material for the play of drama and vice versa.

Verbal dueling is a fascinating speech-play form in which grammatical and lexical play and wit as well as interactional play and strategy are intertwined. Verbal dueling is at the heart of the intersection of speech play and verbal art and reflects and expresses in extremely creative ways the essence of the relationship between and among language, culture, society, and the individual.

Puns, jokes, proverbs, trickster behavior, riddles, and verbal dueling, which are common in everyday conversation, are both playful and verbally artistic. They relate to one another in various ways, intersecting, overlapping, and interpenetrating. Puns can be the punch lines of jokes. Puns and proverbs can serve as witty comebacks. And riddles, as well as puns and proverbs, can be turns in verbal duels. These forms often seem to flow seamlessly within talk and yet are crucial to the strategic interaction which is basic to conversation. While they are often moments or constituents of larger discourse forms, such as conversation, storytelling, or speech making, they can become an elaborate form of discourse themselves, as is the case with joke-telling sessions, riddling contests, and verbal dueling.

These forms of talk and interaction, when contextualized ethnographically, reveal much about a group of people's social, cultural, and personal lives—their systems of beliefs, their daily preoccupations, their relations with others, and the kinds of changes they are undergoing. While these are mainly oral forms, they may have written versions. As the world we live in becomes more and more literate, some of these forms (for example, trickster tales and verbal dueling) are increasingly in danger of disappearing. At the same time, they continue to tell us much about the human spirit and the nature of language in relation to cognition and interpersonal communication.

CHAPTER 4

From Speech Play to Verbal Art

Language—in the general, multifaceted sense—
embodies the intellectual wealth of the people who
use it. A language and the intellectual productions of
its speakers are often inseparable, in fact. Some forms
of verbal art—verse, song, or chant—depend crucially
on morphological and phonological, even syntactic,
properties of the language in which it is formed. In
such cases the art could not exist without the language, quite literally.

> —Ken Hale, "Language Endangerment and
> the Human Value of Linguistic Diversity"

This chapter further develops a view of language structure and language
use as creative, adaptive, and emergent, in which grammar and the sociolinguistic situation provide potentials which are actualized and exploited in discourse, especially verbally playful and verbally artistic discourse. The boundaries between speech play and verbal art are hard to
delimit and are cultural as well as linguistic. At the same time, there are
certain verbal forms where the relationship between the two is particularly salient and where it is quite clear that forms of speech play constitute the building blocks of verbal art. These include most particularly
the stretching and manipulation of grammatical processes and patterns,
repetition and parallelism, and figurative speech. Typically verbal art is
characterized by combinations of these forms of speech play. They may
be used to satisfy the formal requirements of a particular genre—for example, the rhyme and meter scheme of a sonnet or the line structure of
a haiku. Most generally they are used in combination to create, satisfy,
and break the expectations of audiences of oral performances and readers of written texts.

Poetic and literary language is special and different from everyday language, even if it sometimes emerges within and is located within everyday language. What is special and different depends on the particular
language and the particular culture and society. At the same time, there
are widespread general patterns, such as the stretching and manipulation of grammar, the use of repetition and parallelism, and a specialized

vocabulary, including figurative language. The formal properties of poetic language are sometimes and in some places codified in a metalinguistic vocabulary and theory. At other times and in other places they can be discovered only in actual performances of particular genres.[1]

Word Games and Puzzles

I begin with certain forms of speech play which are highly and mechanically structured, so much so that they are often labeled oddities or curiosities and can form the basis of word games and puzzles.[2] They illustrate the potential for language to be used in strictly formal and codified arrangements, a potential which is also crucial to verbal art. Well-known examples from English and other European languages include palindromes, anagrams, acrostics, shaped or emblematic poetry, limericks, graffiti, and echo verse.

Both palindromes and anagrams have a long history in the Western literary tradition. A palindrome is a word or sequence of words that are the same whether read forward or backward. Here are some well-known examples:

A man, a plan, a canal, Panama.
Madam I'm Adam (Adam said to Eve).
Able was I ere I saw Elba (Napoleon).[3]

As a gamelike challenge, palindromes can be expanded into whole verses or poems, as in the following:

PALINDROMIC CONVERSATION BETWEEN TWO OWLS
"Too hot to hoot!"
"Too hot to woo!"
"Too wot?"
"Too hot to hoot!"
"To woo!"
"Too wot?"
"To hoot! Too hot to hoot!"[4]

Anagrams rearrange the letters of a word or longer expression into a new expression related in meaning to the original. Like palindromes, they are miniature, jewel-like genres which are simultaneously secretive, poetic, and gamelike.

Accentuation. I can cut a tone.
Admirer. Married.
The almshouse. A homeless hut.[5]

Acrostics are puzzle-like forms, often poems, in which the words of each line all begin with the same letter of the alphabet or begin with a particular letter, so that the lines spell out a word or name, or progress through the entire alphabet.

WORDSWORTH
Wandering, through many a year, 'mongst Cumbria's hills,
O'er her wild fells, sweet vales, and sunny lakes,
Rich stores of thought thy musing mind distils,
Day-dreams of poesy thy soul awakes:—
Such was thy life—a poet's life, I ween;
Worshipper thou of Nature! every scene
Of beauty stirred thy fancy's deeper mood,
Reflection calmed the current of thy blood:
Thus in the side "Excursion" of thy mind,
High thoughts in *words* of *worth* we still may find.[6]

Shaped poetry visually represents a verbal form on a printed page in such a way that it reflects what the verbal form is about. Compare two versions of several verses of Proverbs 23 from the Bible. The first is represented in conventional linear fashion:

29. Who hath woe? who hath sorrow? who hath contentions? who hath babbling? who hath wounds without cause? who hath redness of eyes?
30. They that tarry long at the wine; they that go to seek mixed wine.
31. Look not thou upon the wine when it is red, when it giveth its color in the cup, when it moveth itself aright.
32. At the last it biteth like a serpent, and stingeth like an adder.

The second example (see Figure 1) represents these same verses in the form of a wine glass.[7]

Shaped poetry has implications for an understanding of the nature of poetry, especially its written representation, and in contrast to other verbal genres. The writing of poetry in the shape of lines stresses the notion of line as basic to poetry, while the writing of prose in the shape of block paragraphs stresses sentences constructed into paragraphs as the essence of prose. The writing of drama with the names of characters fol-

THE WINE GLASS

Who hath woe? Who hath sorrow? Who
hath contentions? Who hath wounds
without cause? Who hath redness
of eyes? They that tarry long
at the wine! They that
go to seek mixed wine!
Look not thou upon the
wine when it is red,
when it giveth
its color
in the
cup
when it
moveth itself
aright.
At
the last it
biteth like a serpent
and stingeth like an adder!

FIGURE I

lowed by their turns at talk stresses conversational interaction as the essence of theater. Experimental writers (of poetry, prose, and theater, and on the internet) as well as translators (of both written and oral literature) are aware of the various possibilities of representing verbal discourse in writing, on a printed page.[8]

Limericks are a highly formalized genre which are at the edges of the boundaries between speech play and verbal art. They are a light verse form of five anapestic lines, of which lines one, two, and five are of three feet and rhyme, and lines three and four are of two feet and rhyme. Limericks are often characterized by certain desirable features. Thus they often contain double (rich) rhymes or near rhymes, such as *Bosham/ wash'em,* and use place-names or persons' names as final words of lines, especially the first line.

There was a young girl from Tottenham.
Had no manners or else she'd forgotten 'em.
At tea at the vicars.
She tore off her knickers
Because, she explained, she felt hot in 'em.

Notice that the phonological pattern of limericks is so marked that if one pronounces only the rhythm in nonsense syllables, it is clearly recognizable as a limerick:

Da da da da da da da.
Da da da da da da da.
Da da da da da.
Da da da da da.
Da da da da da da da.

Limericks were extremely popular in the Victorian era, which saw a tradition of bawdy and obscene limericks that was part of the period's larger tradition of bawdy and obscene literature.[9] Limericks, like jokes, are often told in rounds, and can resemble verbal dueling (this was also true of Victorian-era limericks). And like many other speech-play forms, they themselves can be played with, as in this metalinguistic example:

The limerick form is complex
Its contents run chiefly to sex
It burgeons with virgeons
And masculine urgeons
And swarms with erotic effex.[10]

Graffiti are a public genre which involve written representations on walls of various kinds and in various places. Like many of the forms of speech play discussed here, graffiti have an old, indeed ancient history. Graffiti are often obscene and tend to invite multiple and anonymous authorship. They can become verbal duels in which each author tries to cap the previous one with a stronger and/or funnier comment.[11] Here is an example taken from the wall of a University of Texas building which ends with the expression of a political position:

A billion seconds ago the first atomic bomb hadn't been set off.
A billion minutes ago Christ hadn't been born.
A billion hours ago men still lived in caves.
A billion dollars ago in terms of government spending was this
    morning.

Notice the use of "dollars" in a temporal expression, quite akin to Dylan Thomas's phrase "a grief ago," which I will discuss below.

Echo verse is another ancient form of speech play, dating back to Greek and Roman writers. Traditionally a riddlelike form based on sound play akin to puns, it consists of a question in which the last syllable or syllables are repeated in order to answer the question. Here are some examples:

Question: In a crowded building what shout is the greatest terrifier?
Answer: Fire.
Question: How did the lion feel after devouring the pretty gladiator?
Answer: Pretty glad he ate her.
Question: In what popular sport do you swing your pole low?
Answer: Polo.
Question: What do you say if you stub your toe on the couch?
Answer: Ouch.

While word games and puzzles, verbal oddities and curiosities are seemingly pure play and mechanical manipulation—uncanny manifestations of the plasticity and malleability of language, of both signifiers and signifieds—they are often forms with an ancient history. In addition, they lead us to other forms of speech play, which utilize related formal conventions, and which in many places in the world are highly valued and considered to be verbally artistic.

Figures of Speech

Another ancient tradition consists of creating and formalizing patterns in the arrangement of words as part of the enterprise of verbal persuasion (rhetoric) and/or aesthetics (poetics). These patterns are often called *figures of speech*. In addition to parallelism and metaphor, which I will discuss separately, some examples of figures of speech are antithesis, anastrophe, parenthesis, apposition, ellipsis, asyndeton, polysyndeton, anaphora, anadiplosis, climax, antimetabole, polypopton, and chiasmus. This list is not intended to be exhaustive, since extended and developed treatments of figures of speech can be found elsewhere. Rather, my intention is to place figures of speech within a network of forms and processes relating speech play and verbal art.[12]

Antithesis presents contrasting ideas within a single utterance:

Many things difficult to design prove easy to perform.
Let the rich and prosperous give to the poor and needy.

Anastrophe inverts the usual or expected order of words:

To school you must go.

Parenthesis interrupts the natural flow of an utterance with an inserted phrase:

He tried—who could do more?—to restrain their fury.

Apposition places words or phrases side by side, for purposes of modification or explanation:

Men of this kind—soldiers of fortune, pool-hall habitués, beach-combers—expend their talents on trivialities.

Ellipsis omits words which are implied by context:

When in doubt, play hearts.

Asyndeton omits conjunctions, resulting in a hurried rhythm:

I came, I saw, I conquered.

This is also an example of climax (see below). *Polysyndeton* proliferates conjunctions for purposes of emphasis, solemnity, flow, and continuity:

This semester I am taking anthropology and sociology and linguistics and history and mathematics.

Anaphora is the repetition of the same word at the beginning of successive clauses for the purpose of providing a strong emotional effect:

The Lord sitteth above the water floods. The Lord remaineth a King forever. The Lord shall give strength unto his people. The Lord shall give his people the blessing of peace.[13]

In *anadiplosis* the last word of a clause is also found in the beginning of the following clause:

Hard work is rewarded with success, success leads to prosperity, prosperity produces confidence.

Climax provides a listing building in strength or power toward a conclusion:

Let a man acknowledge obligations to his family, his country, and his God.

Antimetabole is a repetition of words, in successive clauses, in reverse order. Like other figures of speech it is aphoristic and mnemonic:

One should eat to live, not live to eat.[14]
Ask not what your country can do for you—ask what you can do for your country.[15]

Polypopton is the repetition of words derived from the same root:

He is a man to know because he's known.

Chiasmus is a reversal of grammatical structure without the repetition of words:

I am indisposed to work but to beg I am ashamed.

Notice that while these are classical figures, named by specific terms, they are found in contemporary everyday speech as well. They are part of the discursive apparatus, beyond the syntax of sentences, which structures the flow of talk and verbal interaction. Their purpose is to create particular effects with words and groups of words, such as classification, analogy, surprise, insistence, attenuation, intensity, or opposition.

Stretching and Manipulation of
Linguistic Patterns, Processes, and Practices

Given the dynamic (rather than fixed or static) and open (rather than closed) nature of linguistic structure—a point that I stress in this book—various types of stretching and manipulation can occur in language. These are highly dependent on the type of language involved and the speech-play and verbal-art traditions that have developed within them. Stretching and manipulation break both the expectations of normative grammar and the grammar of everyday speech. It would be nice if we could always distinguish the stretching and manipulation of grammatical patterning from the deviation from or breaking of the rules of a language's grammar.[16] The rules of number agreement in English between subject and verb, when broken, yield such ungrammatical utterances as "the men sleeps." Breaking the rules of gender agreement in Spanish yields the ungrammatical *libro buena*. Using the wrong numeral classifiers in Kuna yields the ungrammatical *ko matta-kwen* 'one flat finger' instead of the grammatical *ko ka-kwen* 'one slender finger.' These kinds of examples are generally considered by speakers of languages to be ungrammatical (in a linguistic and not social sense), and not part of the speech-play potential for the creation of verbal art. Despite the consensus about some utterances, however, it is impossible to predict with total certainty which grammatical rules will be playfully and aesthetically stretched and manipulated, precisely because of the creative processes involved in play and art.

English grammar, because of the semi-independence of its morphology, syntax, semantics, and lexicon, allows for a playful fuzziness in the determination of and boundaries between grammatical categories such as nouns and verbs. This fuzziness makes possible various kinds of grammatical manipulation and stretching.[17] Thus in "The man eats the fish," "man" and "fish" are lexically distinguished by their inherent (not overtly marked) semantic properties, such as being human or nonhuman. They are both nouns in large part because they occur in the morphosyntactic environment: "the . . . N." In other morphosyntactic environments these same two words can be verbs: "I fish for salmon, I man the ship." And "man" is the subject of and "fish" the object of the sentence "The man eats the fish" because of their syntactic order, as shown in the contrasting sentence: "The fish eats the man."

This characteristic of English results in a squishy overlap between nouns and verbs as well as between and among other parts of speech.[18] Many words in English can, like *man* and *fish*, be either nouns or verbs, depending on the morphosyntactic environment. Examples are *chair, head, hand, finger, elbow, table, water, rain, snow, nurse,* and *hit.* English speakers do not regard this overlap as particularly playful or creative, but it is part of the inherent play in English grammar and leads the way for more play. Thus we have the slang noun *eats* from the verb *eat*, as in "Let's go get some eats." Nouns and even proper names have a playful/poetic tendency to be used as verbs: "I office across the street," "Let me paper clip that for you," "They helicoptered out," "We're visa-ing," "He was Borked," "Christian Dioring," "We're still doctoring," "I waitress on Monday nights," "This is a song about calling my Mom and having her Western Union me," "You'll go good-old-boying around." Other parts of speech can also move out of their accustomed morphosyntactic positions to another, thereby changing their status as a part of speech. Thus prepositions and question words can be used as nouns: "The ins and outs of things," "It takes seriously not only the *what* that people say but the *how.*"

This property of English, manipulated playfully in everyday speech, is also exploited by such linguistic experimenters as Dylan Thomas and e. e. cummings. A good example is Thomas's often-studied phrase "a grief ago."[19] Just as major classes, such as nouns and verbs, are determined by both their inherent semantic properties (a paradigmatic feature) and their syntactic location/collocation (a syntagmatic feature), smaller classes, such as expressions of time, are determined both paradigmatically and syntagmatically, as well as, sometimes, by phonetic and phonological patterns. The semi-independence of these ways of determining classes or parts of speech enables them to be played off against one another, resulting in such poetic forms as "a grief ago."

The word *grief*, not ordinarily an expression of time, becomes one in the context of "a———ago."[20] In fact, for this expression, as for many such expressions in English and other languages, there is a continuum from the ordinary or mundane uses of semantic time words to the use of others, like *grief*, which take on the meaning of time in this context:[21]

a day ago
an hour ago
a while ago
a cigarette ago
a dollar ago
a grief ago

Thus the meaning of the word *grief* results from the interaction of its paradigmatic features and its syntagmatic locations. Phonetics and phonology enter in as well, since *grief* is a one-syllable word, like many other temporal expressions (such as *day, year, month, week,* and *while*). Thomas's expression "a grief ago" is thus not a deviation but rather an exploitation of various properties of the English language and its grammar.

English grammar can be stretched even more. Thus grammatical classes such as auxiliary verbs, which have relatively little semantic content and function as purely formal devices, can be transformed into lexical items such as nouns, through their placement in syntactic contexts—for example, after possessive pronouns—in which nouns occur. This process of what might be called *reverse grammaticalization* characterizes and organizes e. e. cummings's poem "Anyone Lived in a Pretty How Town."[22] Here are some of the many examples from the poem:

he sang his didn't he danced his did.
they sowed their isn't.

Other European languages provide analogous examples. Spanish creates agentive nouns with the suffix *-ero,* used with nouns or verbs, as in *obrero* 'worker' and *carpintero* 'carpenter.' This leads to playful new forms such as *cevichero* (= one who likes to eat *ceviche*). In Oaxaca, men who hang out on the *zócalo,* the central plaza of the city, in hopes of picking up female tourists, are called *zocaleros*. In central Mexico, the verb *callejonear* (with the default verbal infinitive suffix -*ar*) is used playfully to signify 'walk the narrow-stepped, rapidly descending streets' of towns like Guanajuato, which are called *callejones*. In French, some nouns and adjectives can become verbs by suffixing the verb infinitive marker -*er*. Thus *calme* 'calm' becomes *calmer* 'to calm.' Also, the prefix *de*- is used with verbs to mean 'undo' the verb. Thus *faire* 'to do' becomes *defaire* 'to undo.' While not in any French dictionary I could find, the word *bâche* 'cover' becomes *debâcher* 'to uncover'—a playful neologism derived from these two common morphological processes of French grammar. Also from French, the suffix -*iste*, meaning 'one who,' as in *simpliste* 'one who simplifies things,' has recently been added to the month name *juillet* 'July,' creating the new word *juilletiste* 'one who takes a vacation in July,' which is parallel to both *aoûtien* 'one who takes a vacation in August' and *touriste* 'tourist.' A final French example involves contact with English. French has borrowed the recently created English word *cocooning* along with its meaning 'hanging out at home,' and then created a new French verb, *cocooner* 'to hang out at home,' which deletes the English -*ing* and replaces it with the French -*er*.

Probably the most extreme form of this sort of play is nonsense, often called *jabberwocky* after a famous—probably *the* most famous—example from Lewis Carroll. In this example, the semantic-content words are invented and, while seeming phonetically and phonologically to be English, they are not part of existing English vocabulary, or at least common English vocabulary. In contrast, the grammatical apparatus is perfectly normal and standard, and indeed poetic, because of the use of such words as *'twas*.

JABBERWOCKY
'Twas brillig, and the slithy toves
Did gyre and gimble in the wabe:
All mimsy were the borogoves,
And the mome raths outgrabe.

"Beware the Jabberwock, my son!
The jaws that bite, the claws that catch!
Beward the Jubjub bird, and shun
The frumious Bandersnatch!"[23]

It is interesting that this nonsense poem, which in itself is a form of parody, has been parodied even further by its translation into other languages, using the same principle of nonsense I have discussed here. Here is a French translation:

LE JASEROQUE

Il brilgue: les tôves lubricilleux
Se gyrent en vrillant dans le guave,
Enmîmés sont les gougebosqueux,
Et le mômerade horsgrave.

Garde-toi du Jaseroque, mon fils!
La gueule qui mord; la griffe qui prend!
Garde-toi de l'oiseaiu Jube, évite
Le frumieux Band-à-prend. [24]

Co-occurrence manipulations (playing with the juxtaposition of words or sets of words) create semantic anomalies which are characteristic of much twentieth-century European poetry. Here is a representative example, a line of a Dylan Thomas poem:

A Process in the Weather of the Heart [25]

There is no predicting what aspects of grammar a poet will manipulate. The Chilean poet Pablo Neruda breaks the ordinary Spanish rules of person agreement between nouns and verbs in the opening line of one of his poems, "Me siento triste." [26]

Tal vez yo protesté, yo protestaron.

While *protesté* is the past tense form corresponding to *yo* 'I,' and means 'I protested,' *protestaron* is the form corresponding to *ellos* 'they,' and means 'they protested,' thus conflicting with the *yo* which precedes it. More generally, this poem is an exercise in the interplay of grammatical person, as expressed in nouns and verbs.

The relatively but not absolutely fixed rules of word order in English, along with the independence of lexical meaning and morphosyntax, permit permutations and inversions that are used for both rhetorical emphasis and poetic effect. Dylan Thomas placed prepositional phrases before verbs or verb phrases, as in "The force that through the green fire drives the flower." [27]

English prepositions, their meanings and their syntactic locations, provide another good example of play inherent in language structure.

The same preposition can have different meanings in different contexts, including but not limited to location or direction. Compare the meanings of *at* in the following utterances: "He's at the library," "That's the man I want you to look at," "That's the problem I'm working at." In only the first of these is *at* used in a strictly locative sense. This characteristic feature of English prepositions, together with the sociolinguistically determined judgments of using prepositions in sentence-final position, leads to the following joke, told by one group that considers itself superior to another:

> Man from Texas asks man from Harvard, "Where's the library at?"
> Man from Harvard replies, "At Harvard we don't end sentences with a preposition."
> Man from Texas says, "OK, Where's the library at, asshole."

Other European languages also permit word-order permutation in verbal art. In Spanish poetry and song of various places and periods, word-order shifts are common, often satisfying expectations of rhythm and rhyme. In the following song performed by the Panamanian Osvaldo Ayala, the first pair of lines has a prepositional phrase in final position, while the second pair of lines places the prepositional phrase in prefinal position and the object of the verb in final position—so that *amores* 'loves' rhymes with *corazones* 'hearts' (even though a more normal order would be *yo no tengo dos corazones en mi pecho*). Notice also the repetition of the parallel phrases: *yo no puedo* and *yo no tengo*.

> *Yo no puedo yo no puedo*
> *Continuar con dos amores.*
> *Yo no tengo yo no tengo*
> *En mi pecho dos corazones.*
> I cannot I cannot
> Continue with two loves
> I do not have I do not have
> In my chest two hearts.[28]

In the Colombian copla presented below, the object *l'aritmética* is placed before the verb rather than in its normal postverbal position in order to create the rhyme *enseñaba/multiplicaba*.

> *Un estudiante a una niña*
> *l'aritmética l'enseñaba*
> *y al cabo 'e los nueve meses*
> *la niña multiplicaba.*

A student to a girl
arithmetic was teaching
and at the end of nine months
the girl was multiplying.[29]

I turn now to languages of a quite different type. Edward Sapir's 1921 book *Language* is sprinkled with provocative statements that point to the fascinating ways in which language structure relates to speech play and verbal art. Here is one:

> The structure of the language often forces an assemblage of concepts that impresses us as a stylistic discovery. Single Algonkin words are like tiny imagist poems. We must be careful not to exaggerate a freshness of content that is at least half due to our freshness of approach, but the possibility is indicated none the less of utterly alien literary styles, each distinctive with its disclosure of the search of the human spirit for beautiful form.[30]

What Sapir is referring to here is the polysynthetic structure of an Algonquian language like Fox. Earlier on in this same book he analyzes a Fox verb, *eh-kiwi-n-a-m-oht-ati-wa-ch(i)*, which he translates, relatively freely, as 'then they together kept (him) in flight from them.' Translating more literally, by labeling each of the many morphemes which are strung together here, we have 'then they (animate) caused some animate being to wander about in flight from one another of themselves.'[31] It is the comparison of the literal morpheme-by-morpheme translation with the freer translation that gives us the sense of stylistic discovery.

In Sapir's translations and analyses of Fox, one gets a sense of a high degree of condensation and economy in form-content relationships, of a dense and intense complexity of meanings, tightly packed into a string of grammatical affixes. This illustrative example does indeed seem like a highly wrought and finely tuned miniature work of verbal art. It also gives us insight into Sapir's conception of what has come to be called the Sapir-Whorf hypothesis, in which the relationship to be studied is not grammar on the one hand and thought or culture on the other, but rather a mediation or expression of the language/thought/culture relationship in discourse, especially verbally artistic discourse. Grammar provides the potentials for speech play and verbal art and, through speech play and verbal art, for ways of perceiving and conceiving of the world.[32] I have experienced this same sense of stylistic discovery getting to know another polysynthetic language, Kuna.

The most characteristic feature of Kuna grammar is verbal suffixation. The Kuna verb is characterized by a stem followed by suffixes selected out of a set of at least thirty-five. The traditional grammatical approach to such a language is to group the suffixes into grammatical/semantic classes and to state co-occurrence restrictions and ordering rules among them. The grammatical/semantic classes include tense (past and future), aspect (timing, movement and direction, position), number (plural, many), distributive (also, again), and modality (negative, want to, possible, optative, emphatic). There is also a passive suffix and several suffixes marking clause linkage and subordination, as well as a narrative marker and several derivational suffixes. These verbal suffixes are optional, rather than obligatory, although this distinction is a complicated one, especially from the perspective of speech play and verbal art.

In the first position after the verb stem occur suffixes that can also themselves stand alone as verbs, including the positionals and many of the movement and direction suffixes. Tense and other temporal-perspective suffixes occur in second position, as do some of the movement and direction suffixes. Number and most modality suffixes occur in third position, with clause-linkage markers occurring in fourth position. One of the modality suffixes occurs in fifth position, and the narrative suffix occurs in sixth position. And the optative, emphatic suffix *ye* occurs in seventh position.

Given this general statement of the structure of the Kuna verb, one might imagine that many verbs contain seven or even more suffixes. But in actual practice fewer suffixes are used with each verb than would seem theoretically possible. Each of the many styles and genres of Kuna makes use of the resources provided by this set of verbal suffixes in a particular, unique way. There are interesting relations between and among styles and genres in this regard. Some suffixes have a greater frequency and greater range of meaning in particular styles or genres. *Ye*, which in colloquial Kuna serves an optative and emphatic function, occurs with greater frequency in magical and curing chants, often marking the ends of lines, and serving as an artistic embellishment or frame. This is an illustration of a process which I call the *poeticization of grammar*. Magical and curing chants make use of a relatively small subset of the full set of Kuna verbal suffixes. At the same time, there are suffixes unique or almost unique to this genre that seem to have little or no referential meaning, serving mainly as markers of the magical-curing style. Spoken narration, especially in formal contexts, uses more suffixes per verb than other styles and genres and exploits the full potential set of suffixes more fully.

Still another way to look at the relationship between styles and genres and verb suffixes is to note certain constellations of suffixes which tend to go together in each genre. There are many such constellations.

Kuna verbal suffixes thus have a simultaneous grammatical and socio-cultural function. Furthermore, in addition to marking genres, subgenres, and styles in this way, many of these verbal suffixes, or sets of them, function culturally/symbolically and poetically in other ways as well.[33]

The positional suffixes provide a characteristic example. A set of four suffixes indicates the position of the subject of an utterance, in conjunction with expressing an ongoing activity. The positional suffixes, which are derived from independent verbs with the same meaning, are *ma(i)* 'lying, horizontal,' *kwic(i)* 'standing, vertical,' *si(i)* 'sitting,' and *na(i)* 'hanging, perched.' Like many Kuna morphemes, the positionals have both long and short forms, the long forms having a final vowel that is deleted in certain grammatical, discourse, and social contexts.

In the following examples, I have used parentheses to indicate deletable vowels and dashes between morphemes. I provide both the full, underlying forms and the actual, pronounced forms. The positional suffixes are highlighted in bold.

> *mas(i) kunn(e)* **-si(i)** 'he is sitting eating': *maskunsi*[34]
> *opilumakk(e)-* **na(i)** *-sunto* 'he was (perched in the water) splashing about': *opilumaynasunto*
> *kap(e)-* **ma(i)** *-yop(i)* 'he pretended he was lying sleeping': *kam-mayop*
> *itto(e)-* **kwic(i)** *-sunto* 'he was standing listening': *ittokwicunto*

The positional suffixes are grammatically and semantically related to a large set of movement and directional suffixes. More generally, these suffixes are part of a semantic and cultural orientation to form, shape, direction, and movement that permeates the Kuna language, from grammar to discourse to verbal art.

The positional suffixes are involved in two kinds of markedness relations. First, the positionals themselves are marked with regard to one another in relation to the description of ongoing activities, with *na(i)* being the least marked, followed by *ma(i)*, and *kwic(i)* and *si(i)* being the most marked. That is, in the absence of knowledge of the actual position of the subject of an utterance, its ongoing activity is described as *na(i)* or *ma(i)*.

Second, most and perhaps all verbs have an unmarked positional associated with them, which is the normal position for carrying out the activity described in the verb. Note that this is according to Kuna cultural logic, and not universal logic. The Kuna logically/culturally sleep in hammocks or beds in horizontal positions; a boat is naturally perched on the ocean water; chiefs chant hanging in hammocks; people eat sit-

ting on benches; and the natural/logical/cultural position for talking is
standing, especially in the Kuna gathering house.

> *kap(e)-* **ma(i)** 'he is sleeping (lying in bed, hammock)': *kammai*
> *ua so(e)-* **na(i)** 'he is fishing (perched in boat)': *ua sonai*
> *sakla namakk(e)-* **na(i)** 'the chief is chanting (hanging in ham-
>   mock)': *sakla namaynai*
> *mas kunn(e)-* **si(i)** 'he is eating (sitting on a bench)': *mas kunsii*
> *sunmakk(e)-* **kwic(i)** 'he is talking (standing in the gathering
>   house)': *sunmakkwici*

Note that there is some ambiguity with regard to the unmarked uses
of positional suffixes as to whether or not position is being indicated. In
other words, they are more grammatical than semantic. The positional
suffixes are somewhat metaphorical as well. They are used, as are the
larger class of movement and directional suffixes, even when not literally describing an activity, and are part of the poetic imagination of the
Kuna language.

Given the combined situation of the optionality of these suffixes and
their markedness relations, marked uses, in both everyday and formal
and ritual speech, can be both playful and poetic. Thus, describing someone nodding off while sitting on a bench in the village meetinghouse as
kap-sii 'sleeping, in sitting position,' is quite humorous. Another example comes from a woman talking with a *merki* 'American,' a resident
linguistic anthropologist, after a somewhat harrowing trip at night during which she, her husband, and their young child and the American and
his wife were battered about in a small dugout canoe on a rough sea. The
woman's indication and description of her husband standing urinating
from the about-to-be-docked canoe, silhouetted against the moonlit sky
and open sea, as *winna-kwici* 'urinating, in standing position' is playfully poetic. The description of individuals in a canoe on a mainland jungle river at night—not quite sure where they are and on their way to an
unknown village and a probably difficult experience, trying to sleep,
cold and shivering—is made vivid by means of the suffix *-ma(i):*
owawanmay-mai '(we) were shivering, while lying (trying to sleep).'[35]

The playful-poetic potential of the positional suffixes is exploited in
humorous stories such as "The Agouti Story," a very popular trickster
tale. Crucial lines in the story hilariously contrast the positions and
movements of the protagonists Agouti and Jaguar, as well as things
around them, by means of these suffixes. Here is an example.

> *us oallenatappi ittokwicunto . . . iptakkarsunto . . . arsuntakoe!*
> *arkusku siit.* 'he (Jaguar) stood listening as he (Agouti) was laugh-

ing as he went along . . . he (Jaguar) began (coming) to leave . . .
how could it come falling? it was sitting in place.'[36]

In magical-curing chanting, addressed to representatives of the spirit
world, the almost obligatory use of positional suffixes—as distinct from
their much more optional use in everyday speech—is one of the conventional markers of this genre of discourse, and enters into the poetry
of line and verse marking and parallelism. Furthermore, two or more of
these suffixes are often alternated in parallel lines, involving a slippage
from the grammatical/referential function of the suffixes to a more poetic one. Semantically, the focus on the details of form, shape, and position is a crucial aspect of the magical control so essential to these
chants. Here are some examples from "The Way of the Snake," used to
control a dangerous snake and raise it in the air.

kali mokimakkemaiye 'The vine (snake) is dragging (in horizontal
    position)'
kali piknimakkekwamaiye 'The vine (snake) is turning over (in hor-
    izontal position)'
kaliti mokimakkenaiye 'The vine (snake) is dragging (in hanging
    position)'
kali piknimakkenaikusaye 'The vine (snake) is turning over
    (in hanging position)'[37]

These four lines are the climactic lines of the chant, and reveal a
striking semantic shift with a minimum change of form, in which the
snake moves poetically and actually from a (horizontal) position on the
ground to a (hanging) position in the air, lifted by the specialist as he
chants the lines.

In the symbolic discourse of the Kuna gathering house, which is
highly metaphorical, the positional suffixes have still another function,
each symbolizing different classes of individuals in the Kuna social hierarchy. Chiefs are either na(i) 'hanging' or ma(i) 'lying,' describing their
typical positions in hammocks in the center of the gathering house. The
chiefs' spokesmen are kwic(i) 'standing,' describing the position they
are in when they make a speech. Members of the community at large are
si(i) 'sitting,' which is their position as they listen to the performances,
chants, and speeches of chiefs, village leaders, and others. Here are some
examples from a speech that was given to counsel a new chief, a genre
in which metaphors conventionally intertwine. Various metaphors for
chief—trees, poles, animals, and positional suffixes—co-occur in a
fugue of metaphors. (See the discussion of metaphors below.)

suar icakkwasaar tayleku nunkumai 'A bad pole indeed is lying
  rotting'
akkwaser namaynai 'The spider is hanging chanting'
emit an ittosii 'Now he is sitting listening to me'[38]

The first two examples constitute different ways of describing what
happens when a chief, symbolized here as a spider or a rotting pole or
tree, behaves badly and therefore must be thrown out of office. In the
third example the speaker is referring to the new chief he is counseling,
who is sitting in front of him.

I have examined positional suffixes in Kuna grammar in terms of both
the potentials or resources of a language and actual language usage, in
which the grammatical resources are exploited, indeed stretched and
manipulated. An adequate account of these suffixes involves a focus
on the relationship between grammar, discourse, speech play, and
verbal art.

In addition to the general typological features of languages (e.g., English and Spanish are languages in which morphosyntax and lexicon
are semi-independent; Kuna is polysynthetic), many subtypological features offer possibilities for speech play and verbal art. These can occur
at any level or component of language. Spanish stress provides an interesting example. Stress in Spanish is regularly and predictably penulti-
mate when words end in vowels or the consonants *n* or *s,* and final when
words end in consonants other than *n* or *s.* Exceptions occur for grammatical purposes and are also regular; they are represented orthographi-
cally. So *hablo* 'I speak' contrasts with *habló* 'he spoke.' The Spanish
stress system thus contains a certain degree of inherent play, which is
then further exploited and manipulated in actual discourse. A good example is found in many Spanish songs over a long time period, and including songs in both peninsular Spanish and Latin American Spanish.
Basically, the stress pattern described above is altered in order to fit the
beat of the music, creating a rhythmic tension between the grammatical stress pattern and the musical stress pattern.[39] Thus from a song
written by Federico García Lorca for his play *Bodas de sangre* (The
words in bold have their inherent stress patterns altered as indicated by
the accent marks I have inserted):

Despierte la novia despierte la novia.
*La **máñaná** de la **bodá** la **máñaná** de la **bodá.***
Wake up the bride wake up the bride.
The morning of the marriage the morning of the marriage.[40]

From a Spanish folksong:

Una vieja vale un real
Una **muchacha** *dos cuartos.*
An old woman is worth a real
A girl two quarters.

From a common *salsa* couplet:

Sí señor
Soy **sonero.**
Yes sir
I am the singer.

Another subtypological feature of language which can become verbally playful and artistic is word compounding and, more generally, the
juxtaposition of words. Putting words together creates new meanings
out of their juxtaposition. Some of these are quite mechanical, and seem
natural. The many English expressions that use body parts metaphorically, such as "eye of the storm" and "head of the table," are perfectly
ordinary to speakers and hearers. The large number of such expressions,
however, is an important component of what have been called "metaphors we live by."[41] Many, if not all, languages use body parts in this
way. Thus Indonesian *mata hari* 'eye of the day' means 'sun.' And again,
many, if not all, languages extend the garden-variety use of body parts as
metaphors to usages which are felt to be creatively playful and artistic.
Kuna and other Mesoamerican and Central American languages use
body parts to describe the parts of recently acquired objects such as
flashlights.

In classical Nahuatl, pairs of words were metaphorically coupled and
used in parallel lines of verse. Thus *in atl in tepetl* 'the water the mountain' (= the city), *in impetl in imicpal* 'their mat their seat' (= their
throne, power).[42]

Kuna men and women love to use or even challenge one another to
remember or invent Kuna expressions for objects and activities that
would otherwise be expressed with Spanish or English words, by juxta-
posing already existing Kuna words in new ways. They laugh at such
playful expressions as *kwallu tii* 'oil water' (= kerosene), *san okinoeti*
'that which makes meat red' (= ketchup), and *kaya elieti* 'that which
wipes the mouth' (= napkin). Little kids think it is very funny that they
can use the model of this last example to create *asu elieti* 'that which
wipes the ass' (= toilet paper). Pairs of graded adjectives such as *big/
small*, *hot/cold*, and *wet/dry* can create a playfully expressive extreme
of the first member of these pairs by suffixing *-suli* 'negative' to the second. Thus *pippisuli* 'small-negative' (= enormous). Forms with *-suli* are

characteristic of the expressive play and humor of everyday speech and are not generally found in formal and ritual genres of speaking and chanting.

While Indonesian simply juxtaposes two nouns to indicate their combination (*ibu bapak* 'mother father' (= parents), a process which seems rather ordinary, it also joins words in a more playfully creative way to express newer notions. Thus *bunga uang* 'flower money' (= bank interest).

Still another area in which grammar (including morphology, syntax, and semantics) is intimately related to speech play and verbal art is classification. All languages implicitly and explicitly, covertly and overtly classify objects and activities in the world, and indeed classification is one of the major functions of language. I will focus here on a particular type of linguistic classification fairly widespread in the world: form-shape classification. I begin with the Athapaskan languages, a family of Native American languages whose geographic extension stretches from Alaska to the U.S. Southwest. In these languages, a set of verbs depicting states or motions have different stems according to the form and shape of the noun which is their subject. Thus the verb stem is different for round objects, ropelike objects, solid objects, and animate beings. In a number of these languages, the appropriate classifying stem is purposely altered or misused for humorous effects. A classic humorous routine in Athapaskan Navajo is for someone to enter a Navajo home and, seeing someone sitting there, perhaps appearing somewhat squat, to ask: "What is that round object there?" instead of "Who is that animate person there?" Such play is common in other Athapaskan languages as well.[43] In contrast to Athapaskan languages, in Kuna, which has an elaborate system of form-shape classifiers used in counting, these numeral classifiers are not playfully manipulated—in spite of the Kuna love of verbal play—and to do so is considered by the Kuna to be a grammatical mistake and not at all humorous.[44] This contrasts with the various ways in which the Kuna verbal positional suffixes are manipulated, both playfully and artistically.

Sociolinguistic Perspective

The sociolinguistic repertoire of any community, its heteroglossia,[45] must also be included in a discussion of linguistic potentials for speech play and verbal art. This repertoire includes all of the different varieties of language used in a community: the languages, dialects, and stylistic variation. Sociolinguistic variation is a source of creativity and vibrance, in everyday speech, in spoken and written poetry, and in song and musical performance. It poses a challenge to the status quo, to standard, mainstream ways of speaking, and presents an alternative to conventional ways of expressing things by providing constant and ongoing forms of innovation. This is especially the case when variant forms are juxtaposed to one another.

Truncation

One very common form of stylistic variation involves short or truncated forms, an interesting area in which linguistic structure, sociolinguistic repertoire, and speech play all come together.[46] Many, if not all, languages have longer and shorter forms of morphemes, words, sentences, and forms of discourse, in which the long forms are more formal, ceremonial, ritual, distant, and polite, while the short forms are more informal, colloquial, and intimate.

English, all over the world, deletes or simplifies final (and sometime initial) consonants in informal, colloquial speech, as in *ol* for *old*, *walkin* for *walking*, *er* for *her*. Several words can be grouped together, resulting in forms sometimes resembling polysynthetic languages like Kuna. Thus *whachaduin* for 'what are you doing?' *whadyadu* for 'what did you do?' *whasup* for 'what's up?' *wanna* for 'want to' and *zat* for 'is that.'

In France, a salient aspect of *parler jeune*, the cool, with-it language of the current young generation, includes, along with the use of *argot* 'slang' and words from *verlan* (the most recent and popular play language), a sprinkling of abbreviated, truncated forms. Thus *crad* for *cradeau* 'dirty,' *petit dej* for *petit dejeuner* 'breakfast,' *ordi* for *ordinateur* 'computer,' *ado* for *adolescent* 'adolescent,' *acro* for *accroché* 'drug addict,' *beaut* for *beau frère* 'brother-in-law,' and *trot* for *trottinette* 'scooter' (one of the hottest fads in France today). Popular Spanish—the informal speech of, especially, rural Latin America—involves such truncations as *pa* for *para* 'for' and *doh* or *do* for *dos* 'two.'

Many Kuna morphemes have a long and a short form, the short form resulting from the deletion of a final vowel, and being more informal and colloquial stylistically: *neka* 'house' becomes *nek*; *wala* 'pole' becomes *war*. When several morphemes combine into a single word, we have such contrasts as *taysasulimoka/dachurmo* 'he did not see either.' Balinese achieves the same stylistic effect by shortening words to their final syllable. Thus the four birth-order names, *wayan*, *made*, *ketut*, and *nyoman*, become *yan*, *de*, *tut*, and *man*.

Politeness

Many European languages have two second-person pronouns, one beginning with *t* and the other beginning with *u* or *v*, the *t* form being the more informal and intimate member of the pair, the *v* form being more formal and polite. French provides a paradigm example. The basic rules are quite straightforward. Individuals use *vous* for people they do not know or do not feel close to, in formal situations, and to express politeness. They use *tu* with individuals with whom they are intimate, in informal situations, and with children. The rules are so general that they leave much room for individual play within the system.[47] People will sometimes use *vous* with intimates to express a playful, metaphorical distance. *Tu* is used as an insult for people with whom one usually would be expected to use *vous*. This simple system can also be exploited by poets. A good example is provided in a song by the Belgian song-writer-performer Jacques Brel, in which the last line of every stanza consists of the clause *"Tu vois"* (you see), followed by the syntactic clause/frame *"je vous verb-ais déjà"* (I was verb-ing you already). In the latter clause, "verb" stands for a series of verbs describing the relationship between two lovers, from first meeting, to intimacy, to distance. The contrast and conflict between the two major stages of the relationship is expressed and indeed metaphorized through the switch in these parallel lines, from *tu* in the first clause to *vous* in the second.[48]

In Bali many concepts, especially commonly used concepts such as pronouns, body parts, and ordinary activities, are expressed by two or more Balinese words. Such words are located on a scale from *alus* 'refined' to *kasar* 'coarse,' the refined words being used to address the upper caste and the coarse words being used to address the lower caste. While this system is strictly and indeed religiously adhered to in ordinary interaction, it is blatantly, boisterously, and scandalously manipulated in the comic moments of dance drama and shadow puppetry, so significant in Balinese ritual life. In particular, the translator-clowns in these performances not only perform puns, comebacks, and verbal duels, but also use languages and speech levels inappropriately. They sometimes follow this up by commenting metacommunicatively on each other's breaking of the rules of sociolinguistic etiquette, all within the frame of the comeback and the verbal duel. Here is a typical exchange between Twalén and Werdah, two popular translator-clowns in the shadow-puppet theater.

Twalén: *Baladéwa nyebak.* 'Baladéwa is bawling.'
Werdah: *Da kétoanga ibané ngomong.* 'Don't speak like that.'[49]

The word *nyebak* is *kasar*, and is used here in order to be purposefully disrespectful and insulting when referring to the noble Baladéwa. It is irreverently and outrageously inappropriate. Werdah's response is a metacommunicative scolding of Twalén's sociolinguistic blunder. In what follows, these puppets go on to complain about the way people no longer use appropriate language for nobles. Such metacommunicative commentary and discussion of the language of social caste and class, quite common within the Balinese puppet theater, is a satirical and almost subversive attack on ancient, rigid, and ritual sociolinguistic rules. It is also a humorous reflection of and on a rapidly and radically changing social and linguistic situation within modern, contemporary Indonesia. It is clearly speech play in the service of verbal art.

Code Switching

Code switching is a form of sociolinguistic play par excellence. It involves the simultaneous use of two or more languages, and both reflects and expresses the coming together of speakers of different languages along linguistic borders, wherever they occur in the world.[50] Code switching is a creative way to express emerging hybrid identities and aspirations. For this reason it is common throughout the world. Some of the many examples include Spanish/English in the United States; Arabic/French in France and the United States; Chinese/English in the United States; Balinese/Indonesian in Bali, Indonesia; Mandarin/Taiwanese in Taiwan and the United States; Kuna/Spanish in Panama; Yiddish/English in the United States; Yiddish/French in France; French/Spanish in France; English/Italian in the United States; Sicilian/Italian in Italy and the United States; and Franco Provençal/Piedmontese/French/Italian in the Italian Alps.

Code switching is sometimes given names, by practitioners or others; in either case it can have pejorative connotations. Examples are Spanglish (Spanish/English), Singlish (Singapore English, which switches among English, Malay, and Chinese), and Krenglish (used among Haitians in the United States, it switches between English and Kreyól).

Code switching, like other forms of speech play, engenders further play based on it. Thus speakers with some knowledge of a language will sometimes insert this language humorously into their discourse in their primary language. Thus two pilots, urinating in adjacent stalls in an airport bathroom:

A: I prefer the Tampa route. But that's life.
B: *C'est la vie* (said slowly with a mocking accent, clearly indicating that the speaker does not speak French).

A common form of play based on code switching and mixing is mock language, in which a language—usually one that is characteristic of groups low on the political-economic and social hierarchy of a community—is inserted into the discourse of the dominant language of this same society, in a purposely parodic form.[51] Examples from the use of Spanish in the United States, which is often used pejoratively by non-Spanish speakers, include *hasta la vista baby* and *no problemo*.

Radio announcers on Spanish-speaking stations in Miami mock both Anglos trying to speak Spanish and Latinos trying to speak English in routines inserted between musical selections, framed as though they were phone calls to the station. The following were uttered with a stereotypical American accent:

> *Yo necesito saber cuando yo recojer pastillas para mi vaca.*
> *Yo ordenar* prescription drugs *para las nalgas.*[52]

Analogously, a San Antonio radio station constructs a conversation between a disc jockey and Veronica, a young woman, that is interrupted by her mother. The conversation then turns into a hip-hop song.[53]

V: You know that new song Dr. Dre and M & M?
DJ: Yeah, yeah. You wanna hear it.
M: Hallo!?
V: I'm on the phone.
M: Hallo!?
DJ: Is that Mom? Mom! Hi Mom!
M: Veronica, who you talking to, Veronica?
DJ: Ha, ha. I'm her new boyfriend.
M: Veronica, what'd I tell you bout hanging around, with cochinos Veronica. Hang up the phone.
DJ: I LOVE your daughter.
V: No don't say that.
M: Hang up the phone, Veronica.
V: Mom get off.
DJ: I've been dating your daughter. We're goin out tonight. Zthat alright?
M: Who you talking to? Veronica?!
V: Mom get off the phone.
M: Who ARE you talking to?
V: Ma, get off the phone. You're embarrassing me!
M: How can I be embarrassing you? You needa get off the phone RIGHT NOW Veronica!
DJ: Ha, ha, ha.
M: NO MUCHACHITOS. I tol you they only wan one thing Veronica. Now get in here and clean your room.
DJ: He, he, he.

M: An who'se laughing at me?!

DJ: Ha, ha, ha.

M: Who'se laughing Veronica? HIJA DESGRACIADA! Veronica!!
Wanna these days, HÍJOLE, you're gonna get it!! Wanna these
days get over here right now Veronica!! Why ain't you talking?

V: Get off the phone Mom.

M: Who you calling? Why is this boy laughing?

DJ: Ma'am this is the ra, all she was calling to do wuz make a
request!

V: I just wanna hear a song, why you being so mean?

DJ: Yeah Mm! Chill out a little.

M: WHAT!!!

DJ: She called to make a request!

M: AYY, PERDÓNAME, PERDÓNAME, AYY, QUE MALA, NO!
AYY PERDÓNAME, PER-DÓNA-ME, AYY QUE MALA, QUE
MALAAA!!

V: Get off the phone Mom!

DJ: What, what is Mom saying there?

V: Forgive her, forgive her.

DJ: For forgive her? Oh, you're forgiven! But just don't yell at your
daughter like that.

M: OK, I hang up, Veronica, come clean your room now!

DJ: Ha, ha, ha.

V: Uh, I'm sorry about that.

DJ: Hey, no problem!

Attitudes

Along with sociolinguistic variation and heteroglossia go societal attitudes toward such variation, from both hegemonic and counterhegemonic perspectives. While upper-class and caste elites typically dispar-
age and discriminate against various forms of sociolinguistic variation,
members of communities that use them often feel that humor, vitality,
and expressive exuberance are to be found not in the standard, hegemonic language but rather in the use of local dialects and languages and
nonstandard forms and styles—whether these are Ebonics, Black English, or jive in African American communities in the United States;
code switching or caló 'slang' in Mexican American communities; Yiddish and Yiddish English in Jewish American communities; argot mixed
with verlan in France; the various patois of the European Alps; Venetian,
Neapolitan, Sicilian, and other local languages in Italy; Kuna and other
indigenous languages in Latin America; or local and minority languages,
such as Balinese, within the country of Indonesia.

The sociolinguistic exuberance found in these communities is a source of speech play, humor, and verbal art, as well as resistance to domination by national and standard languages. As in the code-switching examples above, when languages are in contact in communities, the language mix—along with the attitudes toward the languages and what and who they represent—gives rise to play and humor. A hilarious commentary made by a Kuna leader (for example, a chief) after listening to an outside visitor (for example, a Panamanian government official, a Colombian contraband sailor, or an American anthropologist), is *nue shunamakke* 'he speaks well.' The initial *s* of the verb *sunmakke* 'to speak' is ironically pronounced as *sh*, in the manner of the Spanish conquerors, and an *a* is added in before *makke*, turning the form into a ritual one. This is a sociolinguistic joke with five-hundred-year-old roots. The Balinese pun/comeback/routine response to *sudah siap?* 'are you ready?' uttered in Indonesian is *sudah ayam?* 'are you a chicken?' This works because *siap*, in addition to meaning 'ready' in Indonesian, means 'chicken' in the high level of Balinese, while *ayam* means 'chicken' in both Indonesian and the low or ordinary level of Balinese. These examples demonstrate how subtle humor can be and how hard it is to translate from one language and culture to another.

Sociolinguistics and Poetry

In addition to humor, the play made available by the juxtaposition of two or more languages can be used for poetic purposes. In bilingual communities in the United States, forms of poetry have been developed which draw on both of the languages used. One of many contemporary American Indian poets, Ofelia Zepeda, writes poetry bilingually, confronting the reader with a juxtaposition of Tohono O'odham and English texts, even if she or he does not know both languages. These are not translations in the conventional sense, but are acts of transcreation, two verbal forms which evoke one another. Notice that the English version creatively stretches the possibilities of English grammar, using color terms as adjectives, adverbs, nouns, and verbs.

NA:NKO MA:S CEWAGI
CLOUD SONG
Ce:daghim 'o 'ab wu:sañhim.
To:tahim 'o 'ab wu:sañhim.
Cuckuhim 'o 'ab him.
Wepeghim 'o 'abai him.

Greenly they emerge.
In colors of blue they emerge.
Whitely they emerge.
In colors of black they are coming.
Reddening, they are right here.[54]

In Latino communities there are forms of poetry that manipulate everyday code switching between English and Spanish, as well as dialects and styles of each. Here is a pioneering and bitingly satirical poem by Américo Paredes which, like the border folklore he studied so well, mocks and literally turns upside down the way Anglos stereotype Mexican speech and behavior along the Rio Grande in South Texas.

THE MEXICO TEXAN

The Mexico-Texan he's one fonny man
Who leeves in the region that's north of the Gran',
Of Mexican father he born in these part,
And sometimes he rues it dip down in he's heart.

For the Mexico-Texan he no gotta lan',
He stomped on the neck on both sides of the Gran',
The dam gringo lingo he no cannot spik,
It twisters the tong and it make you fill sick.
A cit'zen of Texas they say that he ees.
But then, why they call him the Mexican Grease?
Soft talk and hard action, he can't understan',
The Mexico-Texan, he no gotta lan'.

If he cross the reever, eet ees just as bad,
On high poleeshed Spanish he break up his had,
American customs those people no like,
They hate that Miguel they should call him El Mike,
And Mexican-born, why they jeer and they hoot,
"Go back to the gringo! Go lick at hees boot!"
In Texas he's Johnny, in Mexico Juan,
But the Mexico-Texan, he no gotta lan'.

Elactions come round and the gringos are loud,
They pat on he's back and they make him so proud,
They give him mezcal and the barbacue meat,
They tell him, "Amigo, we can't be defeat."

But efter elaction he no gotta fran',
The Mexico-Texan, he no gotta lan'.

Except for a few with their cunning and craft
He count just as much as a naught to the laft,
And they say everywhere, "He's a burden and drag,
He no gotta country, he no gotta flag."
He no gotta voice, all he got is the han'
To work like the burro; He no gotta lan'.

And only one way can his sorrows all drown,
He'll get drank as hell when next payday come roun',
For he has one advantage of all other man,
Though the Mexico-Texan he no gotta lan',
He can get him so drank that he think he will fly
Both September the Sixteen and Fourth of July.[55]

Rather than follow the quite strict syntactic rules for code switching used in everyday speech, Latino poets invent their own. The results are quite creative, sometimes humorous, and always political. Notice that contemporary poetry, in this case Mexican American poetry, manipulates and stretches not only grammatical and sociolinguistic conventions and norms but also poetic and literary conventions and norms, such as verse design (for example, rhyme and meter) and the placement and representation of a text on a printed page—a concern that contemporary poets share with ethnopoetics. Here is a poem by the activist Chicano poet Alurista, from his *Floricanto en Aztlán*.

WHEN RAZA?
When raza?
when . . .
    yesterday's gone
and
    mañana
mañana doesn't come
    for he who waits
no morrow
    only for he who is now
to whom when equals now
he will see a morrow

mañana la Raza
    la gente que espera
no verá mañana
our tomorrow es hoy
    ahorita
que VIVA LA RAZA
    mi gente
our people to freedom
    when?
now, ahorita define tu mañana hoy[56]

Here is a poem by another activist Chicano poet, Abelardo Delgado. Note that in this poem all the Spanish words are placed in quotes:

EL BARRIO
I am that piece of land "la ciudad" is trying to hide,
I house "gente" to whom the American dream has lied,
in my corners stand the youth "morena" with no future,
in "callejón" walls' graffiti find their nomenclature.
my aroma of hunger brings "muerte" to the table,
Monday's wash on the "tendederos" tells a torn fable
as a "chisme" dripping away from old women's parched mouths,
I act as stereo amplifying clearly "dolor" shouts.
my "calles" shudder littered with the weight of many needs,
my "ambiente" is constant SOS that no one heeds.
I am the alma mater of lost "almas" and bodies,
"yo soy" the unkept laboratory where man studies,
erupting like a volcano "con un" upset stomach
"escupo" the sick, the delinquent, I am a hammock
to the "prostituta," a cemetery to ambition,
a corner to "talento" no exit just admission.
"yo soy el barrio," the slum, the ghetto, progress' sore thumb,
my zombies live "por hoy" and their children have grown pain
    numb,
collectively I am a spirit "que es" explosive,
"yo fabrico" defeat of a quality that's plausive,
conservatively, comfortably "soy casa" of all
who suffer, thirst and hunger, "formando" precious rubble,
I am "humano" my skin absorbs with ease diseases,
through the marrow of my weak "huesos" a rat releases,

playful "cucarachas" and dancing lice, festive pieces
as the barrio readies for "la venida" of Jesus.[57]

Here is a well-known song from the "Tex-Mex" musical tradition
which mixes both musical forms (country western, rock and roll, and
norteño/Tejano) and languages (English and Spanish):

HEY BABY QUÉ PASÓ?
Thought I was your only vato.
Hey baby qué pasó?
Please don't leave me de ese modo.
Come on baby turn around.
Let me see your pretty blue eyes.
Don't you know that I love you?
Please don't leave me de ese modo.
Hey baby qué pasó?
Thought I was your only vato.
Hey baby qué pasó?
Won't you give me un beso?
Hey baby qué pasó?
Thought I was your only vato.
Hey baby qué pasó?
Please don't leave me de ese modo.
Come on baby turn around.
Let me show you how I feel.
Don't you know that I love you?
And my corazón is real.[58]

Poetry based on style shifting and code switching constitutes a political act of consciousness and identity, as well as ethnic, social, and cultural resistance to hegemonic poetic models and, more generally, the ho-
mogenized, monolingual, English-speaking America they represent.
More recently, even more radical experiments in sociolinguistic manipulation and stretching have emerged. Guillermo Gómez-Peña, in his
performance poetry, creates his own form of linguistic, social, political, and individual identity with a sociolinguistically exuberant mix of
Spanish, English, and French; various dialects of each, including standard, nonstandard, and slang; as well as Nahuatl. Here is one of two
"Traditional Boleros" from his *The New World Border: Prophecies, Poems, and Loqueras for the End of the Century.*

BESAME MUCHO
kiss me, kiss moi my chola
como si fuera esta noche the last migra raid
kiss me, kiss moi mi chuca
que tengo miedo perderte somewhere in L.A.

watcha' que maybe mañana yo estare en la pinta
longing for your ass (digo eyes)
y que quizá me deporten de nuevo a Tijuana
por ser ilegal [59]

Along with the poem, Gómez-Peña provides some explanatory notes
that reflect the sociolinguistic underpinnings of his work.

chola = cute
chuca (cf pachuca) = barrio women (in pachuco slang)
ass/eyes pronounced same in Chicano English
pinta = prison

Gloria Anzaldúa adds a gender/lesbian dimension to this mix, as in her
poem "Una lucha de fronteras / A Struggle of Borders":

Because I, a *mestiza*,
continually walk out of one culture
and into another,
because I am in all cutures at the same time,
alma entre dos mundos, tres, cuatro,
me zumba la cabeza con lo contradictorio.
Estoy norteada por todas las voces que me hablan
simultáneamente. [60]

In the following poem, Anzaldúa compares the *mestiza* to corn because of crossbreeding:

We are the porous rock in the stone *metate*
squatting on the ground.
We are the rolling pin, *el maíz y agua,*
la masa harina. Somos el amasijo.
Somos lo molido en el metate.
We are the *comal* sizzling hot,
the hot *tortilla*, the hungry mouth.

We are the coarse rock.
We are the grinding motion,
the mixed potion, *somos el molcajete.*
We are the pestle, the *comino, ajo, pimienta,*
We are the *chile colorado,*
the green shoot that cracks the rock.
We will abide.[61]

Anzaldúa explains her political and sociolinguistic stance as follows:

The switching of "codes" in this book from English to Castilian Spanish to the North Mexican dialect to Tex-Mex to a sprinkling of Nahuatl to a mixture of all of these, reflects my language, a new language—the language of the Borderlands. There, at the juncture of cultures, languages cross-pollinate and are revitalized; they die and are born. Presently this infant language, this bastard language, Chicano Spanish, is not approved by any society. But we Chicanos no longer feel that we need to beg entrance, that we need always to make the first overture—to translate to Anglos, Mexicans, and Latinos, apology blurting out of our mouths with every step. Today we ask to be met halfway. This book is our invitation to you—from the new mestizas.[62]

Mexican American poets and songwriters explore the linguistic hybridity which reflects their cultural, personal, and intellectual lives, and is so well expressed in the titles of their works—Américo Paredes, *Between Two Worlds;* Guillermo Gómez-Peña, *The New World Border;* Gloria Anzaldúa, *Borderlands/La frontera: The New Mestiza.* These examples of bilingual poetry and song enter into a long tradition of multilingual expression in Western poetry and prose, from puzzle and game-like macaronic verse to James Joyce's *Finnegan's Wake.* They are also part of a worldwide phenomenon, as illustrated by Balinese theater.

Contemporary avant-garde poetics, characterized by grammatical and sociolinguistic stretching and manipulation, has been appropriated by such capitalistic endeavors as advertising. It has then been reappropriated and reinvented, further manipulated and stretched, as part of the expression of a poetic/political/ethnic identity by contemporary performers and writers, such as Latino poets and hip-hop and rap musicians and poets. Just as Mexican American consciousness, identity, and resistance to hegemonic political and poetic forms are expressed in bilingual and multistylistic poetry, poetic forms of the African diaspora draw on and manipulate the heteroglossic worlds they emerge from. In Jamaica and Trinidad and Tobago and their diasporic communities, dub poetry, a performed rhythmic genre with strong political messages set to music—in the tradition of calypso and reggae but with links to rap and hip-hop—draws on and manipulates everyday modes of expression, Caribbean slang, and the sounds and feel of words. Like the code-switching poetry of U.S. Latinos, dub poetry is an act of political as well as poetic identity and resistance. The hip-hop and rap poetry, song, and music of African Americans is analogously intended and constructed. One of the pioneers of contemporary African American poetry is Amiri Baraka, whose rhythmic poetry, in addition to its grammatical and sociolinguistic stretching and manipulation, is influenced by jazz beats, represented visually on the printed page.

> BLUDOO BABY, WANT MONEY, AND ALLIGATOR GOT IT TO GIVE
> say day lay day may fay come some bum'll
> take break jake make fake lay day some bum'll
> say day came break snow mo whores red said they'd
> lay day in my in fay bed to make bread for jake
> limpin in the hall with quiverin stick
> he's hiney raised, in a car by the curb,
> licking his yellow lips, yellow snow yellow bubs
> yellow eyes lookin at the dark, hears his whisper
> says, "come down goily i give you a stick . . . da da da
> come down goily i give you a pinch . . . da da da
> come down goily i sit in my car . . . da da da
> come down goily to where we grey guys are . . .
> da da da . . .
> da da da . . .
> da da da . . .
> da da da . . . "
> she's not thinkna him, seein him, seen people like him
> dazed out there, suckin heavy vapors, her butt throw off,
> like stick-it-in nitetime, for the dough, chile, for the money
> baby, look at him down there, lookn up at me . . . da da da
> she and jake
> look[63]

Sonia Sánchez adds a feminine/feminist component to this mix in a poem included in an anthology co-edited by Baraka. Notice again the experimentation with visual representation, including the oral/aural/written interplay which results from the manipulation of orthographic conventions.

TO ALL SISTERS
hurt.
   u worried abt a
little hurting.
           man
hurt ain't the bag u
   shd be in.
        loving is
the bag. man.
       there ain't
no MAN like a
     black man.
he puts it where it is
and makes u
      turn in/side out.[64]

African American expressive language and culture, in particular speech-play and verbal-art forms such as verbal dueling, hip-hop, and rap, are an expression of African American identity, consciousness, and resistance. These poetic forms are characterized by spontaneity; a use of a variety of sociolinguistic styles, including especially African American vernacular; indirection, including puns and metaphors; a powerful metrical regularity together with linguistic details that play with and off of this regularity; musical, especially jazz-inspired, contrapuntal rhythms; a call-and-response interactional pattern; a focus on jive; and, when written, a placement of words and sounds on the printed page intended to visually represent all of this.[65] Here are some examples from the screenplay to *Slam*, an award-winning film dealing with hip-hop and rap in a prison setting. First, by *Slam* poet Saul Williams:

"yo, man you brought me a note?"
what?
"you got a note for me?"
what?
"you can't kick a little rhyme for me?
just a little, man.
i need to hear some lyrics.
i'll make a beat for you."[66]

And, with a feminist component, Jessica Care Moore, from "The Sweetest Revolutionary":

My evening gown is a guerrilla green
I make offerings of myself before the first of every month
'cause there are bills to be paid
instead of getting laid I prostitute verbs manipulate whispers
defined as words
saying shit we've already heard
but not quite like that

See, I know she-poets who'll
squeeze nippled hard headed trees
at their knees
just so their men will name them honey
haikued hips dripping 17 syllables of sweat
drying you off with sunset breath
still he ain't feeling you yet?

Tongue-tied you travel on top of yellow bees
hiding your real sting 'cause he likes the quiet type
cool yeah right-right right-right
you search your belly adjust your skully
hoping to find some sexy sentence hiding between revolution
and rhyme making[67]

The lyrics (and music) of hip-hop and rap offer some of the best examples of the speech play–politics intersection. Here are the opening
lines of Tupak Shakur's "Me against the World." Notice that the transcription, which I found on the internet, aims at reflecting in written
form the sound patterns of African American English oral expression.

It's just me against tha World ooohhhhh ooohhhhh

just me against tha world baby ohhhhhh ohhhhhh

I got nothin' ta lose it's just me against tha world

ohhhhh stuck in tha game

me against tha world baby[68]

Finally, I turn to children's poetry, another kind of poetic act of identity, either written by adults and read to children who listen, read, re-
peat, and appreciate it as theirs, or created by children themselves. This
poetry characteristically manipulates and stretches grammar in ways

quite appealing to children, who are still in the process of acquiring linguistic competence. Here is a characteristic example called tangle-talk, which jumbles syntactic co-occurrence rules. It was recorded from a twelve-year girl.

Twas in the month of Liverpool
In the city of July,
The snow was raining heavily,
The streets were very dry.
The flowers were sweetly singing,
The birds were in full bloom,
As I went down the cellar
To sweep an upstairs room.[69]

In the following, verbs are punfully made out of the names of fruits and vegetables.

Do you carrot all for me?
My heart beets for you.
With your turnip nose
And your radish face
You are a peach.
If we cantaloupe,
Lettuce marry,
Weed make a swell pear.[70]

Repetition and Parallelism

Repetition and parallelism are often considered to be the most basic principles underlying verbal art. And in fact, repetition and parallelism, of many types and at all levels of language, are extremely widespread in the verbal art of many societies, as well as in ritual and ceremonial language (which is often considered to be verbally artistic). The pathbreaking theorist of parallelism as the governing principle of poetry is Roman Jakobson, who developed and illustrated his approach in a series of papers.[71] Jakobson's focus was on grammatical and semantic parallelism, as will be mine here. He started from the basic opposition between the paradigmatic and syntagmatic axes of language and demonstrated that parallelism results from projecting the paradigmatic axis, that of selection or choice, onto the syntagmatic axis, that of arrangement. While Jakobson drew his examples mainly from written poetry, parallelism based on the interplay of the paradigmatic and syntagmatic axes of language enables both oral and written speech play of all kinds, including rhyme, meter, puns, spoonerisms, and humorous and clever comebacks within everyday verbal interactions.

> (A customer in a taxi apologizes to the driver for forgetting that one
>   of the back doors does not open.)
> Customer: I'm a slow learner.
> Taxi driver: But you might be a late bloomer.

> A bank teller verifies the identity of a customer over the phone
>   before giving him an account balance:
> What is your social security number?
> What is your date of birth?
> What is your mother's maiden name?
> What is your grandmother's blood type? [72]

Repetition and parallelism are always present in language. All of language can be conceived of as the interplay of sames and differences, and the task of a linguist is to analyze these, at all levels. The issue for us here is: What play or verbally artistic use is made of this potential for repetition that goes beyond linguistic structure, creating not just grammatical sentences but poetic and rhetorical movements and figures?

While parallelism, in its most elaborate form, is characteristic of highly marked ritual and poetic language, it can also be found in other verbal events, those not usually considered verbal art. Examples include the following excerpts from two related American press conferences, both having to do with the hottest political issue in the United States at the end of the twentieth century. In the first, a well-known political personality, Vernon Jordan, is talking about his relationship with President Bill Clinton.

> Let me reassure you that ours is an enduring friendship, an endur-
>   ing friendship based on mutual respect, trust, and admiration.
>   That was true yesterday. This is true today. That will be true
>   tomorrow.[73]

Notice two types of parallelism here. First there is a looser, general one. This is manifested in the repetition of the phrase "enduring friendship" and in the listing of items, from the same semantic field, following one another: "respect, trust, and admiration." Second, there is a stricter grammatical and semantic parallelism. Here, two paradigms (verbal

tense and the temporal adverbs *yesterday, today, tomorrow*) are combined in the generation of three parallel sentences, based on the model
"That X (tense of the verb *to be*) true Y (day)."

That	was true	yesterday
This	is true	today
That	will be true	tomorrow

In the second press conference, an ex-presidential aide who has just
been indicted promises not to testify against the president, by saying the
following:

> The Office of Independent Counsel can indict my dog. They can
> indict my cat. But I'm not gonna lie about the president. I'm not
> gonna lie about the first lady.[74]

This statement is constructed out of two pairs of parallel utterances.
The first uses the frame "can indict my X" and pairs *cat* and *dog*, the two
most common pets in American society (and often associated with one
another, as in the proverbial expression "It's raining cats and dogs"). The
second uses the frame "I'm not going to lie about X" and pairs the first
couple of the United States government: the president and the first lady.

In addition to the poetic effect of these examples of parallelism, they
have a rhetorical effect as well. The rhetorical effect of Jordan's use of
parallelism is that of movement in a particular direction (yesterday, today, tomorrow), and is an example of the rhetorical figure of climax (see
above in this chapter for a discussion of figures of speech). Since these
two statements are not manifestations of formalized, codified, conventional genres, the parallelism involved seems emergent, rather than
frozen or fixed.

In the United States, parallelism is characteristic of both political and
religious rhetoric. Here we find their intersection in a speech by Jesse
Jackson at the 2000 Democratic convention. Parallelism underlies phonetic rhyme and morphological and syntactic structure, resulting in a
humorous but politically powerful statement:

> This democratic convention is set in that great divide.
> Between Beverly Hills and South Central.
> Between the dream makers and dream breakers.

In Western written literature, repetition is often considered to be
redundant and boring. In contrast, it is often highly valued in Native
American oral discourse. Many forms of verbal art in Native America,

especially those used in ritual and ceremonial contexts, are structured through the repetition of sounds, words, phrases, lines, and verses. This structure moves performances along, provides an incantatory tone, and aids in the memorization of fixed verbal forms as well as the creative performance of flexible or adaptable verbal forms. Performances often involve the repetition of a frame, within which there is variation. Here is a small portion of the Navajo "Blessing Way," a curing chant, which ensures health and well-being.

Earth's feet have become my feet
    by means of these I shall live on.
Earth's legs have become my legs
    by means of these I shall live on.
Earth's body has become my body
    by means of these I shall live on.
Earth's mind has become my mind
    by means of these I shall live on.
Earth's voice has become my voice
    by means of these I shall live on.
Earth's headplume has become my headplume
    by means of these I shall live on.[75]

The aesthetic coherence and unity of these lines is created by the exact repetition of the line "by means of these I shall live on," which alternates with the parallel lines generated by the frame: "Earth's [body part] has become my [body part]."

In Mesoamerica and lowland, tropical South America, parallel couplets, extensive lists, and the stacking of poetic lines are quite common, indeed characteristic of the public oral performance of verbally artistic discourse. In Mesoamerica, the metaphorical couplet, which was a major organizing principle of the verbal art of the classic Aztec and Mayan civilizations, is a linguistic expression of the dualistic mode of thinking noted in these civilizations. In the words of Miguel Leon-Portilla, the foremost scholar of Aztec and Mayan literature:

Anyone who reads indigenous poetry cannot fail to notice the repetition of ideas and the expression of sentiment in parallel form. Sometimes a thought will be complemented or emphasized through the use of different metaphors which arouse the same intuitive feeling, or two phrases will present the same idea in opposite form. A few examples will make this clear. In an Aztec poem which exalts the Sun, Huitzilopochtli, who is invoked by priests and people alike, the same thought is expressed twice:

From where the eagles are resting,
from where the tigers are exalted . . .

And the parallelism reappears in the same poem singing the great-
ness of Mexico-Tenochtitlan:

Who could conquer Tenochtitlan?
Who could shake the foundation of heaven? [76]

Couplets, as well as triplets, are characteristic of the poetic structure of the classic Mayan epic, the *Popol Vuh*. Here is an example from a speech in which the gods who are the makers and modelers of human-kind call upon older gods who are diviners and artisans to help them:

So be it, fulfill your names:

Hunahpu Possum, Hunahpu Coyote,
Bearer twice over, Begetter twice over,
Great Peccary, Great Tapir,
lapidary, jeweler,
sawyer, carpenter,
Maker of the Blue-Green Plate,
Maker of the Blue-Green Bowl,
incense maker, master craftsman,
Grandmother of Day, Grandmother of Light. [77]

In lowland, tropical-forest South America, extreme parallelism is characteristic of curing chants which communicate with representatives of the spirit world. Here is an example from the Suyá Indians of Mato Grosso, Brazil, of a curing song for a child with fever:

1. Blowing [physical blowing]
2. Master of the still waters
3. Master of the still waters
4. Master of the still waters
5. Master of the still waters
6. Master of the still waters
7. Rough-skinned white cayman his hand is spread out. How come?
8. Animal, Animal, that lies there still.
9. Master of the still waters
10. Master of the still waters, white cayman
11. Master of the still waters, with his rough skin, lying there in the stream,
12. Master of the still waters

13. Master of the still waters
14. Master of the still waters
15. Master of the still waters
16. Master of the still waters
17. White cayman, master of the still waters
18. His hand is spread out, his neck skin is spread out, his hand is spread out, he trembles not. How come?
19. Animal, animal, lying there
20. Master of the still waters
21. Master of the still waters
22. Master of the still waters[78]

Anthony Seeger, who recorded this chant, analyzes its parallel structure:

> There is a structure to the curing song, involving a parallelism between certain parts. This curing song can be divided into six parts as follows:
>
>   A: lines 1, 2, 3, 4, 5, 6
>   B: lines 7, 8, 9
>   C: lines 10, 11
>   D: lines 12, 13, 17, 15, 16
>   E: lines 17, 18, 19
>   F: lines 20, 21, 22
>
> There is a structural parallel between A, C, and F (repeating the phrase "master of still waters"), and also between B and E. This leaves lines 10 and 11 as a kind of pivot. The lines are part of the central core of the song, and they combine both the name of the animal and the mastery of the still waters. The lines thus represent a synthesis of AB/DEF.[79]

There are many types of parallelism in the verbal art of the Kuna Indians, involving phonology, morphology, syntax, and semantics. Parallelism is closely tied to line organization and structure, in that it sets up correspondences based on and cutting across lines and units composed of lines, such as verses. The result of all of these types of parallelism is a slow-moving narration that advances by slight changes in referential content, which are added to repeated information. Extreme attention is paid to minute and precise detail.

The parallelistic structure of curing and magical chants in particular involves all levels, from the most macro—repetition of whole verse and stanza patterns—to the most micro—repetition of words and morphemes. A representative illustration of the complex use of parallelism is the chant *pisep ikar* (The Way of Basil). This magical chant, addressed to the spirit of the basil plant (named *inapiseptili* in Kuna magical, ritual language), is used to ensure success in the hunting of wild animals in the jungle. The hunter bathes in a potion made from the fragrant basil plant and has this chant performed for him by a specialist.[80]

"The Way of Basil" is a verbal mosaic of intersecting and overlapping repetitions as well as parallelistic patterns of all kinds. I present here the opening portion of the chant, which deals with the birth (symbolically described) of the basil plant. In my representation of the text I highlight the grammatical and semantic/lexical parallelism by lining up and stacking parallel words and affixes under one another.

> *inapiseptili olouluti tulalemaiye*
> *olouluti tulallemaiye*

> *inapiseptili olouluti sikkirmakkemaiye*
> *olouluti sikkirmakmamaiye*

> *inapiseptili olouluti wawanmakkemaiye*
> *olouluti wawanmakmainaye*

> *inapiseptili olouluti aktutumakkemaiye*
> *olouluti aktutulemainaye*

> *inapiseptili olouluti kollomakkemaiye*
> *olouluti kollomakmainaye*

> *inapiseptili olouluti mummurmakkemaiye*
> *olouluti mummurmakmainaye*

> That Inapiseptili in the golden box be lying moving
> In the golden box be lying moving

> That Inapiseptili in the golden box be lying swinging from side to side
> In the golden box be lying swinging from side to side

> That Inapiseptili in the golden box be lying trembling
> In the golden box be lying trembling

> That Inapiseptili in the golden box be lying palpitating
> In the golden box be lying palpitating

That Inapiseptili in the golden box be lying making a noise
In the golden box be lying making a noise

That Inapiseptili in the golden box be lying shooting out
In the golden box be lying shooting out[81]

The pervasive patterns of repetition and parallelism, which are particularly characteristic of the structuring of ritual forms of Kuna discourse, result in an interesting tension between form and content. While patterns of parallelism can frame and highlight, thus enhancing and foregrounding referential content, overlapping and intersecting patterns of repetition and parallelism can overwhelm and almost obfuscate referential content. (Note the interesting parallel here between Kuna oral discourse and the *mola*, or woman's blouse, the principal form of Kuna visual art.[82])

Figurative and Metaphorical Language

No discussion of the relationship between speech play and verbal art is complete without dealing with figurative language in general and metaphor in particular. Figurative language, in the form of proverbial expressions, is often crucial to the operation of puns. It can play a role in the structure of jokes as well. Ultimately all of culture and all of language, through which culture is expressed, created, and transmitted, is symbolic and therefore figurative and metaphorical. Metaphor is the basis of all language use in that we use concrete sounds to express idealized meanings—that is, the word *cat* cannot scratch and the word *dog* cannot bark. There is no question that in any language metaphors are omnipresent, and that metaphors are a way not only of talking but of thinking about the world.[83]

Metaphors state an equivalence between terms taken from separate domains; they enable us to talk about one kind of thing in terms of another kind of thing.[84] They work—that is, are understood and are effective linguistically and culturally—because there are both similarities and differences between the domains they relate. Metaphors can have quite different manifestations in different languages and cultures. They are cognitive in a cultural sense.

All languages and cultures have metaphors that people live by, in the sense that they organize and orient many objects, thoughts, and activities that people are engaged in and talk about. Examples from English include temperature (hot/cold), animals, color, direction (up, down, in, out), and body parts. Body parts are extremely rich and complex in metaphorical development. They are extended to bodylike objects or objects that can themselves be conceived of metaphorically as bodies. Thus *the head of a nail, the leg of a table,* and *the spine of a book.* Certain objects of clothing have parts named for the part of the body they touch. Thus pants have legs and crotches and shoes have heels, soles, and toes. Social organizations are structured in terms of body parts: *head of a family, strong arm of the association.* Many locations, activities, skills, emotions, and relationships are expressed through body-part metaphors: *eye of a storm, heart of the matter, have a heart, two-faced, save face, cold shoulder, knuckle down, put your finger on it, green thumb, all thumbs, bosom buddy, tongue-tied, on the tip of the tongue, tight-lipped, stiff upper lip, lip service, keep your chin up, skin deep, ear for music, in one ear and out the other, stick out one's neck, shoulder the load, hands are tied, lead someone by the nose, slap in the face,* and *stab in the back.* Both body-part metaphors and metonyms are used for individuals, often derogatorily—heel, prick, asshole. Other European languages have similar extensive metaphorical uses for body parts. Among the Apaches and other Native North American groups, human body parts were first extended to the horse and then to the automobile.[85]

While metaphors can usually be thought of in terms of lexical or vocabulary relations and replacements, some are located in the grammatical heart of a language. In most indigenous languages of Mesoamerica, nominal postpositions which indicate the location of an object are derived metaphorically from body-part nouns. Thus *stomach* signifies 'in,' 'inside', or 'under'; *heart,* 'inside'; *face* and *mouth,* 'to,' 'at,' 'from,' or 'in'; *back,* 'behind'; and *head* or *hair,* 'on' or 'on top of.' Here are some examples from Mixtec, a language of Mexico. What in English is expressed as "He is on top of the mountain" is in Mixtec, literally, 'He is located the mountain's head.' English "in front of María" is in Mixtec 'María's face.'[86]

Many cultures relate human and animal domains through metaphors. These are often a reflection of an agricultural, rural, nontechnological past or present. Here is a typical example, from the island of Tobago, in Tobago creole.

> *Yo mot a go ron like a parrot.* 'Your mouth is going around like a parrot' (= you talk too fast).[87]

Metaphors Kuna live by include plants and animals from the nearby jungle environment and the architectural structure of Kuna houses, as well as movements and positions of various kinds. Among the Kuna there is also constant metaphorical inventiveness, a sign of the vibrancy and adaptiveness of their culture. New words to express new objects in

Kuna culture, especially those acquired from the non-Kuna outside world, are often derived and created metaphorically by the nominalization of an already existing Kuna phrase, usually with humorous effect—one more example of play being humorous but deeply serious as well.

Metaphors, like all aspects of language, are actualized, activated, created, and modified in the context of their use in discourse. Like grammatical patterns and lexicon, they are part of the resources that people use in conversations, arguments, political speeches, and jokes. Thus they are aspects of the poetic and rhetorical organization of speech events. The Kuna use metaphors, in addition to everyday conversation, in two distinct types of ritual discourse: the magical chants which are central to curing and the speeches and chants of the gathering house, the site of political meetings. In magical and curing chants, the metaphors are fixed, and so are part of the memorized text of the chant. They are an aspect of the specialized, esoteric vocabulary known only to the performers of these chants and the spirits to whom they are addressed. They reflect the Kuna belief system and can be playful and humorous as well. Some examples are *kwaki otimakke* 'gather heart,' which means 'think'; *mola* 'Kuna blouse,' which means 'leaves'; *inna ipet* 'owner of chicha' (the fermented drink consumed by the Kuna during certain rituals), which means 'Kuna person'; *kurkin* 'hat,' which means 'brain power'; and *aipanne* 'swing back and forth,' which means 'walk'.

Gathering-house discourse, especially the chants of chiefs, employs a distinct set of metaphors from magical and curing discourse. These are translated and interpreted by the chiefs' spokesmen for the audience. These metaphors include *tuttu* 'flower' for 'woman,' *kalu* 'stronghold of animals' for 'village,' *yala* 'mountain' for 'world,' and *pap kinki sayla* 'Father/God's rifle' for 'thunder.' In addition, sets and networks of metaphors are developed and elaborated on in the course of chants and speeches. For example, the poles and other features of the structure of traditional houses are used as metaphors for political leaders: the main, central pole is the chief, the secondary poles are the chiefs' assistants, and the thatch walls are ordinary citizens of the community. This metaphor, which is used verbally, is also actualized visually when members of a village meet in the gathering house, with the chiefs in the center, surrounded by their assistants, who are in turn surrounded by the men and women of the village.

Metaphors can also be innovated and personally developed or even invented, again in a discourse context. It is such metaphors that are often considered new, fresh, and creative, especially in the context of Western literature. But individual creativity in metaphor use can be found in traditional societies as well. Thus a Kuna speaker—in particular, a chief demonstrating his chanting or speaking abilities—will, in counseling a new chief, often compare chiefs to trees in the jungle. But there are many trees, and the ones he selects metaphorically describe the kinds of chiefs he is talking about. Thus he may choose the *ikwa* tree, a tall, hardwood tree, to describe a chief who is strong and long-lasting but perhaps a bit stingy. Or he may choose the *isper* tree, which yields abundant sticky fruit, to describe a chief who is generous, perhaps a bit too much so. And these metaphors can be adapted to particular situations and personally played with, creatively modified. Thus a pole in a house can become partially rotten, invaded by bugs, and then taken down, the rotten part cut away. After a while, if the pole seems strong and healthy again, it can be used again. A description of this situation can be used to counsel a chief who was thrown out of office for bad behavior but, because he is still knowledgeable in Kuna tradition and a respected leader, has been reinstated once again as chief.[88] Metaphors thus become narratives and narratives, metaphors. And conventions become innovations and innovations, conventions. Such is the nature of metaphor in language.

Metaphors, of course, are in many societies invented by individual performers and poets, and are at the heart of individual creative expression in language, evoking nature, culture, aesthetics, and politics. One of my favorites, in the form of a simile, is Federico García Lorca's *La noche se puso íntima, como una pequeña plaza* 'The night became intimate, like a small square.' This is a beautiful way of expressing the intimacy of both a Mediterranean night and a Mediterranean square.

Metaphors, like proverbs, and, ultimately, all speech play, can be manipulated to humorous ends. The hottest turn-of-the-century drug, Viagra, has become an overnight source of many new metaphors. Here are two, both from serious news media:

> Fellow-travelers find Holbrooke's brand of revisionism so hot a commodity that, not surprisingly, it is being ingested, Viagra-style, in anticipation of a prospective intervention in Kosovo.[89]

> (Talking about Hillary Clinton running for the Senate in New York) It would be Viagra for the media.[90]

How It All Works Together

Grammatical stretching and manipulation break the expectations of normative grammar and the grammar of everyday speech, as well as the expectations of established poetic and literary canons. Parallelism and metaphor, each in their own way, create new expectations and satisfy them. This interplay of the breaking and satisfying of listeners' and readers' expectations is a basic characteristic of verbal art. It is what Roman Jakobson recognized as "the human sense of gratification for the unexpected arising from expectedness, both of them unthinkable without the opposite."[91] Here are some examples.

In the e. e. cummings poem "Anyone Lived in a Pretty How Town," there is a pervasive use of grammatical stretching of various kinds. These include the treatment of indefinite pronouns such as *anyone, someone,* and *everyone* as if they were proper names; the treatment of auxiliary forms such as *did, didn't,* and *isn't* and quantifiers such as *all* as if they were nouns; lines that have no verb but rather a string of nouns from the same semantic field; the treatment of inanimate nouns such as *noon* and *snow* as if they were animate; the treatment of intransitive verbs as if they were transitive; the use of nonsense words such as *dong* and *ding;* and the use of prepositions neither in prepositional phrases nor as parts of verb phrases where they normally occur, but rather in anomalous expressions such as "down they forgot." As various authors have observed, however, while these stretchings might be viewed as deviations from usual English grammar, they are rule governed in the context of this poem.[92] Actually, they are not deviations at all, but rather fascinating explorations in the creation of meaning through grammatical manipulation and metaphor making.

At the same time, there is pervasive and overlapping parallelism in the poem, so that certain grammatical stretchings and manipulations, as well as metaphors, are repeated and thus expected. Satisfied expectations are then broken by means of stretchings and manipulations from the new norm, so that there is a dynamic pattern of interplay of creating, satisfying, and breaking expectations through parallelism. Here is the full poem, with line numbers added for reference.

Anyone lived in a pretty how town
(with up so floating many bells down)
spring summer autumn winter
he sang his didn't he danced his did

Women and men (both little and small)   5
cared for anyone not at all
they sowed their isn't they reaped their same
sun moon stars rain

children guessed (but only a few
and down they forgot as up they grew   10
autumn winter spring summer)
that noone loved him more by more

when by now and tree by leaf
she laughed his joy she cried his grief
bird by snow and stir by still   15
anyone's any was all to her

someones married their everyones
laughed their cryings and did their dance
(sleep wake hope and then) they
said their nevers they slept their dream   20

stars rain sun moon
(and only the snow can begin to explain
how children are apt to forget to remember
with up so floating many bells down)

one day anyone died I guess   25
(and noone stooped to kiss his face)
busy folk buried them side by side
little by little and was by was

all by all and deep by deep
and more by more they dream their sleep   30
noone and anyone earth by april
wish by spirit and if by yes.

Women and men (both dong and ding)
summer autumn winter spring
reaped their sowing and went their came   35
sun moon stars rain[93]

Examples of sets of parallel lines are the following:

(1) lines 1, 17, 25: "Anyone lived in a pretty how town," etc.
(2) lines 4, 7, 14, 18, 20, 35: "he sang his didn't he danced his
   did," etc.
(3) lines 3, 8, 11, 21, 34, 36: "spring summer autumn winter," etc.
(4) lines 13, 15, 28, 29, 32: "when by now and tree by leaf," etc.

An excellent example of a pattern that is created, modified, broken,
and re-created with parallelism is the paradigm of seasons (line 3); which
is replaced with the paradigm of celestial bodies plus rain (line 8); repeated again with the seasons, but in a different order (line 11); repeated

again as celestial bodies plus rain, but in a different order (line 21); repeated as the seasons, now in a third order (line 34); and finally repeated as celestial bodies plus rain, this time in the same order as in line 8 (line 36).

Another pattern, which can be symbolized as "A by B and C by D," starts with two adverbs connected to two related nouns (line 13); switches to two nouns (or a noun and a verb) connected to a noun (or a verb) and an adverb (or a noun or verb) (line 15); then an adjective (or adverb) repeated that is connected to a verb form repeated (line 28); then an adjective repeated that is connected to another adjective repeated (line 29); and, finally and perhaps the most anomalous, most radically breaking expectations set by previous lines, two nouns (or two verbs) connected to the connective "if" and the affirmative "yes" (line 32). Notice also that the pattern "A by B"—with A and B usually the same word, without being conjoined to another "C by D"—is found in line 12; line 27, just before its full use in line 28; line 30, just after its full use in line 29; and line 31, just before its full use in line 32.

The pattern "he verbed his did (or didn't)" (line 4), is found in line 7 with the verb "is" in the negative and the adjective "same," in line 14 with two nouns, in line 18 with a plural noun and then a singular noun, in line 20 with an adverb (in a plural form as if it were a noun) and a noun, and in line 35 with a gerund and a verb form. This parallel paradigm explores different types and degrees of syntactic and semantic anomaly.

In sum, the grammatical stretchings, invented metaphors, and semantic anomalies in this poem are counterbalanced and given cohesion by the extreme parallelism. The interplay results in dynamic tension because of the constant innovation and surprise against the backdrop of repetition.

In the experimental and humorous Texas-Mexican border song "La ventana sónica" (the sonic window), standard Spanish words are converted into nonsense *esdrújulas*, words in which the antepenult syllable is stressed. The invented words occur at the end of each line and have the forms *-ico* or *-ica* suffixed to them, resulting in a play-language-like effect. The simultaneous manipulation of the stress pattern (phonology), word structure (morphology), and vocabulary creates a pattern which becomes the model for the parallelistic structure of the song.

En una ventana sónica,
divisé una muy bonítica,
componiéndose los rizíticos,
mirándose en el espejítico.

Through a sonic window,
I perceived a very lovely girl,
arranging her curls,
looking at herself in the mirror.[94]

My final example is a song written and performed by the Belgian song-writer-performer Jacques Brel, "J'Amais" (I loved), Here is the song, with the last line of each stanza—an important focus of the song as well as my discussion of it—represented in French as well as English.

I used to love fairies and princesses.
That I used to be told do not exist.
I used to love fire and tenderness.
You see I was dreaming of you already.
[*Tu vois je vous rêvais déjà.*]

I used to love the towers high and wide.
Where one could watch for love coming from the open seas.
I used to love the towers of the guard.
You see I was watching for you already.
[*Tu vois je vous guettais déjà.*]

I used to love the rippling crest of waves.
The noble willows languishing toward me.
I used to love the curling line of the seaweed.
You see I was knowing about you already.
[*Tu vois je vous savais déjà.*]

I used to love to run until I fell.
I used to love the night until dawn.
I used to love nothing no no I adored.
You see I was loving you already.
[*Tu vois je vous aimais déjà.*]

I used to love the summer for its storms.
For the lightning on the roof.
I used to love the flash of lightning on your face.
You see I was scorching you already.
[*Tu vois je vous brulais déjà.*]

I used to love the rain drowning space.
And the hazy mist of lowlands.

I used to love the fog chased by the wind.
You see I was weeping for you already.
[*Tu vois je vous pleurais déjà.*]

I used to love the vines and hops.
The northern towns the ugly ones.
And deep rivers calling me to bed.
You see I was forgetting you already.
[*Tu vois je vous oubliais déjà.*][95]

This song is about the interplay of distance and closeness, formality and intimacy, all metaphorized by sets of nouns within semantic fields, a progression of verbs, and the use of the second-person pronouns *tu* and *vous*. Each stanza consists of a semantic field or paradigm of nouns, the unifying feature of which is summarized in the verb of the final line of the stanza. Thus "fairies and princesses" > "dream"; "towers," "guard" > "watch"; "storms," "flash," "lightning" > "scorch"; and "rain," "mist," "fog" > "weep." The verbs crescendo from *rêver* 'dream' to *aimer* 'love,' and then decrescendo to *oublier* 'forget.'

Grammatical, more precisely sociolinguistic or verbal-interactional stretching is focused on the *tu/vous* interplay. Under normal circumstances, one uses one or the other of these two second-person pronouns at one time, based on the nature of the relationship between the speaker and the addressee—*tu* for intimacy and *vous* for distance. In this song, in the lines in question, both *tu* and *vous* are used at the same time, thus metaphorizing the tension of the interplay between intimacy and distance in the relationship.

The song contains various instances and types of repetition and parallelism. *Aimer* in its imperfect form *j'aimais* 'I used to love' is repeated in the opening of the first and third lines of every stanza, except for, significantly, the third line of the last stanza. Also significantly, it occurs in every line of the focal fourth stanza. This imperfect form *aimais* is contrasted semantically and morphosyntactically with the preterit form *j'ai adoré* 'I adored' in the third line of this very important fourth stanza.

The strictest parallelism is that of the fourth line of every stanza, projecting two paradigms simultaneously: the paradigm of second-person pronominal sociolinguistic choice between *tu* and *vous* within each line, and the paradigm of verbs of relationship, from "dream" to "forget," across otherwise identical lines of the form "You see I was *verb-ing* you already."

The overall result of this interplay and interlocking of grammatical and sociolinguistic stretching, metaphor, and parallelism is a verbal and musical display of the history of a relationship or the singer's portrayal of the relationship, with its ambivalences and tensions, intimacies and distances, and loving and forgetting.

What do anagrams and palindromes, limericks and echo verse; graffiti; jabberwocky; poems by Dylan Thomas and e. e. cummings; bilingual poetry in English and Spanish by Chicano activists; songs by the Texas Tornados and Jacques Brel; hip-hop, rap, and slam poetry and song in the African diaspora; Balinese shadow-puppet plays; children's poetry; and Native South American myths and magical chants have in common? What are they doing together in the same chapter of a book?

My point is precisely to demonstrate, by means of a series of juxtaposed examples, that all of these forms, patterns, and processes are indeed related. While some are more gamelike than others, some are written and some are oral, some are serious and some are humorous, some are sacred and some are profane, some are statements of personal identity and some are intensely political, they all share, each in their own way, an interplay and intersection of basic principles of speech play and verbal art—in particular, grammatical stretching and manipulation, repetition and parallelism, and figurative and metaphorical language.

Because language use is so intimately related to the culture and society in which it is located, verbal forms which involve the interplay of speech play and verbal art—including verse design, metrics, rhyme, the use of pause in oral speech and the representation of sounds and words on a printed page in written speech, grammatical and sociolinguistic stretching and manipulation, parallelism, and metaphor—are all ideological acts and expressions of identity and affiliation. These can be hegemonic or counterhegemonic, reinforcement of a particular power structure or resistance to it, serious political commentary or humorous parody.

CHAPTER 5

Contexts for Speech Play

[T]he study of verbal art can and must overcome the
divorce between an abstract "formal" approach and an
equally abstract "ideological" approach. Form and
content in discourse are one, once we understand that
verbal discourse is a social phenomenon—social
throughout its entire range and in each and every of its
factors, from the sound image to the furthest reaches
of abstract meaning.
   —Mikhail M. Bakhtin, *The dialogic imagination*

There are many ways to conclude this exploration of speech play and
verbal art. I have decided to do so by examining the contexts for speech
play in locations from which I have drawn examples for this book: the
United States, France, Latin America, Panama (among the Kuna), and
Bali, Indonesia. By *context* I mean both the immediate and concrete situations and settings in which speech play occurs, including the social-
interactional strategies involved, and the general assumptions and ideologies underlying the practice of speech play. Through an examination of
these places and contexts, and the significance of speech play in and for
them, I propose a final argument for the importance of the study of
speech play and verbal art more generally, in the light of an intersection
of theoretical approaches to both language and culture that have become
salient as we enter the twenty-first century.

The United States

In general, speech play in North American society represents a contrast
with and break from the serious stuff of life. The many examples I will
present here should be familiar to readers who have participated in or
experienced similar or analogous moments of speech play. My purpose
is to contextualize them in various ways.

Play and Games

A common context for speech play in American society is the playing
of games, from cards to tennis. While play and games are quite different,

and games can be very serious, both play and games constitute, for most people, time off and time out from economic transactions and activities. For this reason games lend themselves to speech play. Speech play is furthermore time out and time off from the seriousness and official rules of games. The play frame is a frame or frame break within the game frame.[1] Here are some examples.[2] Notice that in addition to playing with and breaking frames, these instances of speech play (like all of the examples I provide in this section) often involve forms which I have examined in other chapters, such as proverbs and proverbial expressions; puns; grammatical stretching and manipulation; metaphors, parallelism, and other poetic and rhetorical devices; and verbal skidding and dueling.

> During a card game being played in an airport by a group of people waiting for a plane, one of the players says, "I don't mind losing, I just hate when someone else wins."

> At a dog sled race, a woman who is there to watch the races asks a racer who is walking with his sled, "What kind of wood is that?"
> The racer responds, "Birch."
> The woman comments, "I burn that in my fireplace; it burns real well."
> The racer: "That's what I'll do to it tonight if I don't race well."

Here are a series of examples taken from the game of tennis.

> During a doubles match in tennis, a member of one team "hogs" a shot from his partner and misses. In response, one of the opposing players yells out, "Oink oink."

The animal sound metonymically labels the player who (like a pig) stole the shot.

> In a tennis doubles match, one player says to his partner, whose play he has not been happy with, "It wasn't a personal comment when I called you a creep, Charlie, it was an observable fact."

Here is one that tennis players will no doubt appreciate.

> After winning a point, following which a ball rolled over from another court onto his, the winning player says to his opponent, "Did that ball bother you?" When his opponent responds, "No, it came after the point," the winner of the point responds, "I meant the one I hit."

This is classic trickster behavior, of the kind found in puppet shows like *Punch and Judy* and Marx brothers movies. Similar banter occurs in the next tennis examples:

> A ball rolls onto a court from the next court over and the two play-ers decide to replay the point. The person who is responsible for hitting the ball over says, "I'm sorry," to which the person who lost the point to be replayed replies, "Thanks for saving me."

> After hitting two balls onto a neighboring court simultaneously, a player says to a player on the other court, "You've got two of ours" [meaning "please return them"]. The player who has the two balls that don't belong to him replies [breaking the tennis etiquette frame], "I'll keep them."

> A man leaving the tennis courts passes behind a court with two people playing. One of the players hits a ball way out of the court. The passing player asks the man who has just won the point, "You need help with that call?"

> After a player wins his third game in a set of tennis, he draws on and manipulates a well-known proverbial expression by saying, "A cat has nine lives. I just got my third."

> While playing tennis, two individuals are carrying on a discussion of football. One points out that big guys get hurt the most. The other responds with the proverb "The bigger they are the harder they fall."

A final tennis example uses a common expression in the world of sports to describe the relationship between marriage and tennis. Notice the rhyme and parallelism.

> A woman says with regard to herself and her husband, "We don't play together so we can stay together."

Television and Radio

Television and radio sports announcers are fond of playful interjections as part of their otherwise referential descriptions and discussions. Here is a TV announcer describing the tackling of a quarterback in a football game:

He's huggin him but he's not lovin him.

Another TV announcer describing a tense moment in a baseball game, the final game of a playoff series:

In this crowd there's enough adrenaline to liven a corpse.

Finally, a TV announcer characterizing what happened to a baseball player who had gone 0 for 6 and then drove in the winning run:

It's the epitome of going from the doghouse to the penthouse.

Speech play on television and the radio is not limited to sports. Here a local radio announcer in Austin, Texas, describing an upcoming event in the town of Burnet, pronounces it "Burnét," stressing the second syllable. He then corrects himself, repronouncing the town as "Búrnet," stressing the first syllable, and says the following, with playful poetic rhyme and rhythm:

It's Búrnet dúrnet. Why can't you learn it?

These last two examples are an appropriate way to end this section, in that they combine so many of the forms of speech play that have been the subject of this book: metaphor and figurative/proverbial speech, repetition and parallelism, frame manipulation, and punful play on words.

Everyday Conversation and Interaction

Speech play, including frame breaks, also occurs in everyday conversation and verbal interaction. Practiced by men and women, young and old, and people of all professions and walks of life, it is adapted to their age, situation, and the social context. Here are some examples:

A nurse says to a woman who has just entered a hospital requesting immediate care, "You have to be a little patient." The woman responds, "I'm a big patient."

This verbal play is based on the fact that the word *patient* can be either an adjective or a noun.

A tennis player who had just gotten an old-fashioned crew cut and had practically no hair on his head walks onto a tennis court to begin a match. A man on the next court, a total stranger to the entering player, asks him, "Wha'd you do? Tell the barber an ethnic joke?"

A man enters an airplane and says to a passenger seated in the middle of a row, "The good news is you're comfortable, the bad news is I'm there" (pointing to the window seat).

A young girl who works as a lifeguard at a neighborhood pool walks into the men's room at the end of the day in order to clean it. As she enters she says in a lilting voice, "Knock knock. Anyone in the men's room?"

Notice how the form of a knock-knock joke is combined with a request, thus making the request playful.

A woman in a gas station says to the owner of the station, while asking him to send out someone to fix a flat tire, "I don't know what's wrong with that tire. It's flat as a pancake."

The metaphorical comparison of a flat tire to a pancake renders this example playful and humorous.

Two men in a parking lot are trying to stick a wire through the window of their locked car. A passerby asks them if the key is locked inside. One of them replies, "No, I just like standing in parking lots trying to stick a wire inside my car."

The frame break here is based on this being a response rather than a reply to the question.[3] Here is another example of a frame break based on a humorous response rather than a true answer to a question. It involves a very common, almost formulaic comeback.

One person asks another, "Did you watch the football game last night?" The other responds, "Is the Pope Catholic?"

Another formula commonly used in such contexts is "Is there snow in Alaska?"

The next example plays with and partly constructs the social identity of the participants involved:

Two elderly gentlemen, residents of a retirement home, are standing outside their building deciding what to do next. One of them observes, "Don't spend all your money. Save it for your old age."

Here is a conventional metonym for describing one's belongings, permanent or temporary:

> A group of people are traveling in a shuttle bus from an airport to a remote parking lot. They are asked by the driver to identify their cars. One of the riders says, "I'm the green Buick."

This example is similar to a customer's announcement to a waiter or waitress arriving with several plates: "I'm the enchilada verde."

Between close friends, speech play can take the form of mock insults bordering on a verbal duel, as in the following, which was followed by laughter:

> A: Why didn't you bring us some donuts? (said to a man entering a room eating a donut).
> B: Go get them yourself.
> A: Shut up, Richard.[4]

Here is a playful, collaborative verbal duel based on body parts.

> A mother and her young daughter are in the parking lot of a supermarket. A passerby asks them, "Do you have the time?" The mother responds, "12:30 on the nose." The mother and daughter walk toward the supermarket and the daughter says, "On the mouth," to which the mother replies, "On the ear," and they both laugh.

This duel begins with a recognition by the daughter of the humorous arbitrariness and metaphorical properties of the expression "on the nose" and becomes the kind of speech play characteristic of children's and child-adult verbal interaction. Children in American society love speech play. In fact, adults often consider speech play to be by and for children, and a marker of adulthood is precisely not engaging in the sorts of speech play associated with children. The next example is typical:

> A large group of young children are running around the aisles of an airplane. One of them says, "Watch out, it's a children jam."

This example plays with and manipulates the expression "traffic jam." In the context of children, adults feel comfortable using speech play, as the next example demonstrates:

When first-class boarding is announced to a group of people waiting to board their plane, a young boy runs toward the gate. His
mother says, "Where are you going? We're not first class." A man
standing beside them but not related to them says, "Yes you are."
Taking up the playful verbal duel, based on the double meaning
of "first class," the woman responds, "In everything else we are."

Children use speech play as a resource in their struggle against, resistance to, and sparring with adults, especially parents, as the next quite
typical example of children's sarcasm illustrates:

A young girl walks toward a set of tennis courts with so many
objects in her hand that she cannot open the door to the courts.
She says to the adults (probably parents) with her, "Thanks for
holding the door open for me."

Finally, there are frame breaks which playfully transform ordinary interactions between two individuals into mock transactional ones, making a nice point about the relationship between speech play and the serious stuff of life in America, which often has do with economic gain.
Here requests for free goods are transformed playfully into economic
transactions:

A man in a crowded airport is waiting for his plane to depart. He
notices a place between two individuals already seated and asks
them, "Is this free?" One of them responds, "Yes. . . . No, it costs
twenty dollars."

A student enters a university office and asks a staff person working
at the front desk, "Can I borrow your stapler?" She responds,
with a straight face, "That'll be fifty dollars."

Two individuals are together in a university laboratory. One of them
says to the other, "Is that your paper?" (a conventional American
way of requesting permission to take a nonvaluable item, in this
case a newspaper). The other replies, "You can have it. Just leave
a dollar at the door on your way out."

Here a similar simple request is rejected:

A customer in an automobile repair shop asks an individual working at his desk, "Can I use your phone?" He responds, "No."

This blunt, abrupt, impolite response is inappropriate except in play. It was followed by a granting of permission to use the phone. In the following example, such mock transactions are themselves mocked:

> A woman, having just walked through the streets of New York, enters an apartment building where she has been invited for dinner. She sits down in the lobby and begins to change her walking sneakers into her dining shoes. She says to the watching doorman, "I am just going to change my shoes," to which he responds, "That will cost you extra."

Transactions

These mock transactional examples lead nicely to the next set of examples, which involve speech play within the small talk characteristic of such transactional settings as waiting in line, checking out of a store, or cashing a check in a bank.[5] The humor of this speech play is based on a surprise momentary break in frame, followed by a return to the transaction. In addition to drawing on such conventional or classic forms of speech play as puns, repetition and parallelism, and proverbial expressions, these playful misrepresentations often take the form of banter, comebacks, and side sequences.[6] Here are some examples.

> In response to a request for service, a library clerk says to a patron, "We'll see what we can't do for you."

> After ringing up the charges to a customer in a supermarket, the cashier says, "That will be three thousand five hundred and twenty-four pennies."

> A travel agent on the phone with a client, summing up what she has just done: "That way I complete the loop. I know that you know that they know that I know about the reservation."

Here is a manipulated proverb used humorously:

> A doctor asks a patient who has come to see him because of back pain if his back hurts, and the patient says that it does not hurt now but that it did in the morning, and that coming to see the doctor made the pain go away. The doctor responds, "Benjamin Franklin said, 'God does the healing and the physician collects the fee.'"

Here is a favorite *Alice in Wonderland* character put to use:

> A speaker at a public hearing, arguing against a local development project, summarizes by saying, "This is Humpty Dumpty."

Here are several comeback routines:

> A potential customer enters a small hotel in a small western country town and says to the owner, who is working at the front desk, "Do you serve breakfast?" to which the owner, instead of a blunt "no," responds, "I have a deal with eggs. I don't beat them and they don't beat me."

> A man accompanies his elderly mother to a driver's license office to obtain a driver's license to use as an identity card. The mother explains to the clerk at the desk, "He's my son. He's driving me." The clerk responds, "He's driving you crazy."

> An airport attendant is helping a man on a plane to get into a wheelchair in order to be wheeled off the plane. He asks the man, "Can I move you a little further back?" The man responds, "Yes, so you can earn your fifty thousand dollars." The attendant responds, "It's only forty-nine thousand, nine hundred and ninety-nine."

This kind of banter with numbers, which once again reflects American society's concern with real economics, is characteristic of both Punch-and-Judy-like puppet shows and the theater of the absurd.[7] This is precisely why these art forms, popular as well as literary, are funny—they draw on and indeed imitate common everyday speech play. The following example of verbal banter involves a pair of comebacks:

> A man is in line at a supermarket service counter to return empty bottles and get his deposit back. Inadvertently he bangs the bottles against the counter. A woman in line behind him says, "Watch out, he's dangerous," to which he replies, "It's the company I keep," thereby indicating their relationship (probably husband and wife).

Here the comeback occurs over the phone:

> A man calls a store to find out if it is open. When the phone is answered, he says to the person who answered, "I was just calling

to see if you were open. You obviously are." The person who
answers the phone responds, "No, we're closed," and then laughs.

Here is a comeback uttered by one professional to another, in the pres-
ence of a client/patient.

One dental hygienist instructs another who is working on a patient,
"Start on the right side." The other responds, "I always start on
the other side. I'm a communist."

Here it is the customer who is joking:

A customer in a bank gives a fifty-dollar check to a teller and asks
him to cash it. The teller asks, "How would you like that sir, two
twenties and a ten?" The customer replies with a straight face:
"In hundreds."

Airplane Humor

Even the serious settings of boarding and giving instructions on an airplane can be the locations of frame-breaking speech play. The play and
humor of these examples is heightened by the fact that they flirt with
danger, since messages from pilots and attendants are typically quite
referential and serious, and by law one cannot joke about or even allude
to such matters as having weapons on an airplane or bringing weapons aboard. In fact, the following announcement is quite common in
airports:

Any inappropriate remarks or jokes may result in your arrest.

Against this backdrop, the following are even more humorous:

Security agent to passenger: Please bring your bag over here so we
can check it.
Passenger: I have a tape recorder in there.
Security agent: I'm not checking the bag, I'm sniffing it.

She then laughs at her own allusion to the use of dogs to sniff for drugs
in airports.

A gate agent at the Houston, Texas, airport announces over a loudspeaker the departure of a plane to Austin during the legislative
session: "All passengers going to Austin please board at this

time. All Democrats, Republicans, and independents please board at this time."

A stewardess is explaining over a loudspeaker to passengers in a plane what to do if oxygen masks automatically come down. She says, "You first give yourself oxygen and then your husband."

As a flight is about to take off, a flight attendant says, "Welcome to flight 6. If Austin was not in your flight plan today, it is now."

A flight attendant in the middle of instructions to passengers, apparently repeating a serious routine, says, "If this flight turns into a crash, your life jackets are under the seat in front of you."

Shortly after that he announces, "We'll be dimming the lights in the cabin to provide that special ambience and to increase the attractiveness of the person sitting next to you."

As the plane taxies to the gate he says, "Keep your seat belts fastened until the captain has turned off the Fasten Seat Belt sign. We have never had a passenger reach the terminal before the aircraft and we'd like to keep it that way. Anything left on board will be split among the flight attendants."

Pilot, apologizing for a late departure due to a mechanical repair, announces (in an antimetabole-like structure) to the passengers, "It's better to be on the ground wishing you were in the air than in the air wishing you were on the ground."

Flight attendant, as she wheels a beverage cart through the aisle of the plane: "Watch your knees, your nose, your toes, and your elbows."

Note how the structure of this warning is based on classic forms of speech play—the repetition of four body parts after the repetition of the possessive pronoun "your," the first two with alliteration of the initial sound n; the rhyme of "nose" and "toes"; and the breaking of expectations of rhyme, assonance, and syllable structure in the final body part, "elbows." The next two examples reflect and comment on sociolinguistic situations.

Two agents are boarding passengers on a plane departing a gate in the Houston airport. One of them announces in Spanish with a

very marked English accent, "*Pasajeros en filas once y adelante*
'Passengers in rows eleven on.'" The second agent comments,
"Show-off." To which the first says, now in English, "That's the
only Spanish I know."

This interchange is a humorous metalinguistic commentary about language use in the American Southwest, in particular Spanish/English
bilingualism. It is humorous because the agent speaking Spanish did not
speak at all well and was not showing off but doing his job. The following example is a nice parallel case.

> At a gate at the Vancouver, Canada, airport a Chinese Canadian
> agent switches from English to Mandarin in talking to a col-
> league, and another (non-Chinese) agent says, "That's easy for
> you to say."

Greetings

A common location for speech play in American society is greetings.
In order to understand why, it is useful to begin with Erving Goffman's
extended and provocative discussion of greetings, which he calls "sup-
portive rituals."[8] According to Goffman, since "social nature abhors an
empty slot,"[9] greetings have to occur. Basically anything that occurs in
the greeting slot, the "access ritual" slot—usually the opening of an interaction or the only part of an interaction—will be produced and interpreted as a greeting. This includes not only verbal utterances, but also
gestures, eye contact, smiles, and, most relevant to my discussion here,
play, joking, and laughter. Since greetings essentially involve the filling
of empty slots (but slots that are extremely important ritual slots, from
a social-interactional point of view), and since speech play, as I will ar-
gue below, provides grease and oil for social interaction in American society, speech play occurs quite naturally in greetings. In fact, greetings
are often the site of convivial and public speech play. Here are some
examples.

> A woman sees a neighbor talking to electric-company workers as
> she pulls out of her driveway in her car. She opens her window
> and calls to the neighbor, "Hi John. Have you changed jobs?"

> A man enters a plane. Another man who is already seated greets
> him as he walks by, saying laughingly, "They let anyone on these
> planes."

A man shopping in a supermarket sees an acquaintance and says, "Hi Mike." The acquaintance puts his hand on the man's shoulder and says, "You meet the funniest people in the funniest places."

A secretary greets her boss as he walks into the office with a loud and surprised voice: "Hi, hi, hi." The boss replies, "Mary no less."

An optometrist comes into the waiting room of his office and greets his next patient with this playful insult: "Beth, come on in." Turning toward the receptionist he adds, "Oh my god. Anybody but her. I don't allow street people."

Two friends and neighbors who live in the same apartment complex pass one another. One says, "Hi Bob, what's up?" The other replies, "Nothin."

It is interesting that this greeting between two acquaintances resembles a common Kuna-greeting interchange:

One Kuna passes another on the streets of a Kuna village and says, "*Anna*" (a nonreferential equivalent of English 'hi'). The other person responds, "*suli*" ('no').

Back to American society:

A young girl carrying a plastic bag approaches a boy in a university gymnasium. Both seem to be students and both are laughing. The boy says, "Whacha doin with that?" The girl responds, "I'm a bag lady."

Public greetings in particular can be playful. Some express ethnic and (socio)linguistic identity, as do forms of public handshakes. Here are some observed among African Americans, although not necessarily restricted to this ethnic group. Note the use of names and terms of address.

Man to woman on a street: "Whass up Redbone?"

Woman to woman in the lobby of a hospital: "Hey Kissypooh. Whass going on girl?"

> On the street of a large American city, one man walks up to another
> whom he knows and says, "Can it really be, Johnny G."

This greeting has the rhythm and rhyme we associate with poetic structure, in a playful frame. Play with names is common also in the comeback banter which can occur in greetings.

> In a university office one individual sees another whom he has not
> seen for a while. He says, "Hello Mary Jane Smith." She replies,
> "Hello James Jones."

The humor here starts with the use of the full name by the first greeter
and is continued by the parallelism used by the second. This sort of play
can also happen on the phone:

> A caller says, "William, this is John again," to which the person
> being called responds, "Hello John again."

Another telephone example:

> The caller says, "Sam, it's John calling you back." The person being
> called responds, "Hello John calling you back."

Deictic utterances, in the third person, are often used as playful humorous greetings:

> A guard, standing at the door of a university library, greets two
> women entering the library by saying, "There go my two favorite
> ladies."

> Two individuals pass one another and one says, "Look who it is,"
> and the other responds, "Here she is."

> Two individuals are seated in front of a university building and see
> a third person whom they know walking toward the building. All
> three are smiling at one another. One of the seated individuals
> says, "Look at Ms. Coordinated Professional." (The color of her
> dress matched the color of her bag.)

Just as greetings provide a common location for speech play, related
interactions, such as introductions or beginnings of events, are appropriate for speech play as well, especially as a way of repairing interactional
or communicative mishaps or embarrassments.

At an academic conference, a panel chairwoman introduces a
speaker who has mistakenly left his paper on the lectern. She
sits down, taking the paper by mistake. She then apologizes,
saying, "I took your paper by mistake," to which the speaker
responds, "Why don't you read it for me," and both laugh.

A professor walks into his class and there is a newspaper on the
lectern where he usually puts his notes. He says to the class,
"Did someone leave this for me?" After a few embarrassing
moments of silence one of the students says, "Yes, it's for you,"
and then laughs and says, "I was only kidding."

Greetings after long or significant absences are more exuberant than
mechanical everyday greetings, and can involve speech play, along with
other verbal and nonverbal actions.

A mother gets off a plane in an airport with her young son and finds
her husband waiting with a baby. The four of them hug, kiss, and
laugh in a bubbly greeting.

Two individuals, because of the accident of suddenly or surprisingly
running into each other a short time after having seen and greeted
one another, often feel obliged to once again greet. These "second greetings," perhaps because of the sudden embarrassment involved, seem to
have an even greater propensity to be playful and humorous than the initial ones.[10]

A university-department faculty member has just greeted a staff
member in the main office of the department and then sees her
again in the mail room. She says, "Hello," with a loud and mocking intonation.

Two individuals who know one another from sight only pass in the
halls of a university building and one of them says, "Hi." A short
time later they pass again in the doorway to a flight of stairs and
simultaneously say to each other, "Hi again," with smiles and
slight friendly laughter.

Two professors who know one another slightly pass each other on
a university campus. One says, "Hi, how are you?" The second
says, "Fine thanks, how are you?" and the first responds, "Fine."
An hour later they pass again. The first smiles and the second
says, "Again," with a smile.

> A pharmacist in a large store sees a customer with whom he has
> already conversed walking through the store for a second time
> and says (with a smile), "Still walking around."

Here is a case which hovers between a first greeting and a second
greeting.

> Two individuals are in line checking out of a store. A few min-
> utes later they enter another store nearby and run into a woman
> who was in line behind them in the first store. When she sees
> them, she asks in a loud, lilting voice, with a smile, "Y'all fol-
> lowin me?"

Sometimes second greetings are directly metacommunicative.

> A staff member finds himself in the men's room at a urinal next to
> a colleague whom he has passed several times in their office. He
> says, "We meet again."

> Two individuals who have not seen one another for a long time
> meet in the main office of a university department and greet with
> a handshake. They then pass one another several times in the
> office. A few minutes later they run into one another entering a
> door leading to a stairway and one of them says, with a smile,
> "Oop, we meet again."

> Two individuals who had just greeted each other in an office run
> into one another on a flight of stairs. One says to the other, "We
> see each other again," and then laughs.

These second greetings take on added poignancy when the first greeting
occurred after a significant absence.

> An individual, while driving his car, realizes that a person on a bike
> right next to him at a stop sign is someone whom he knows well
> and has not seen for some time. They greet. A few hours later
> they run into one another again in the stacks of a university
> library. One laughingly says to the other, "I saw you already
> today."

As in playful first greetings, third person deixis can be involved in these
playful second greetings:

> A student greets a professor in his office after having seen him in the hallway a short time before by saying, "There he is."

> Two individuals who have already greeted in one university building pass each other in another building, and one says to the other, "Here he comes."

> Leave-takings, like greetings, can also be playful and humorous.

> In a post office a customer ends his encounter with a clerk by saying, "See you," to which the clerk responds with the stereotypical, clichéd leave-taking comeback, "Not if I see you first," which he follows with a mocking "Ha ha ha."

A final example:

> Two students are conversing outside on a university campus. One says, "I gotta go. I have a class in social reaction to crime. I'll commit a crime if I don't go," to which the other responds, "Go ahead and react to the crime."

Of the various societies I examine in this chapter, the United States, in its turn-of-the-century, late-capitalist stage, is the most focused on and oriented to language and interaction as referential and transactional, especially in economic terms. And yet, as the many examples I have provided illustrate, speech play is common in everyday life in America. Speech play, including reframings of various kinds—like the small talk more generally in which it is embedded—provides the lubrication, the oil or grease for verbal interaction. Here it is put very well, in the form of a mock proverb voiced by one dental hygienist (A) to another (B), in response to a small-talk apology that had just been uttered.

> A: Apologies are what make the world go round.
> B: What?
> A: Apologies are part of the oil that greases the world.

Presumably the "world" A is referring to is the place she knows best, U.S. society. From buying things in stores to cashing checks in banks, to making business deals, to making speeches in state legislatures, to making announcements on airplanes, to visiting a doctor, to advertising—while referentiality and transactions are at issue in all these interactions, the wheels of serious talk are greased with speech play. And in a modern, urban, complex society such as the United States, speech play also aids in the anonymous comings together of individuals and groups, cutting across social, ethnic, economic, and gender differences, often for transitory moments and purposes. Thus, speech play serves the serious, the transactional, the economic stuff of life, or else it is relegated to children, comedians, or joke-telling sessions—all of which, in their own way, are time out, time off, or time along the way to the serious stuff of life in American society. At the same time, speech play is enjoyed and valued, and in this sense adds an additional layer of meaning to interactions. Saying of someone that he or she "has no sense of humor" is a serious critique. Speech play also occurs in written literature, which is on the border between the serious and the unserious, the referential/transactional and the diversionary.

Speech play in American society, as well as in others, must be approached in terms of an intersection of two perspectives:

1. Its location and function in social interaction—that is, its role in greetings, leave-takings, introductions, getting the floor, thank-yous, and acknowledgments of thanks.
2. Its patterning as a cultural focus in sociocultural context, including social organization, cultural values and symbols, and ideology.[11]

From the point of view of ideology, it is interesting to note that against the backdrop of a professed, indeed advertised belief in a homogenizing egalitarianism, fairness, and lack of conflict in American society, there is in actuality a great deal of diversity and hierarchy, tension and animosity with regard to gender, class, ethnicity, and language, especially from the point of view of minority and subaltern groups. This confrontation of the ideal and the actual produces a need for a verbal practice of friendship, which is achieved through small talk and speech play. It is interesting that this verbal practice is often viewed as hypocritical by outsiders and the less favored, and is mocked by such groups as Native Americans and African Americans.

And of course, since American society is not homogeneous, speech play patterns differently across its heterogeneity. Its function as lubrication of referential and transactional interaction is an aspect of the dominant, the hegemonic, the mainstream discourse in American society. We get a much different perspective when we look at minority and subaltern groups within the United States—Native Americans, African Americans, Latinos, Italian Americans, or Jews, for example. Each of these groups, in unique and distinct ways, uses speech play to construct ethnic and social identity, express counterhegemonic resistance, and gain covert prestige. At times such speech play leads to misunderstandings, miscommunications, and conflicts with representatives of the dominant, mainstream society, from school teachers, to social workers, to doctors, to the police.

A major source of speech play in the United States emerges from the large network of languages, dialects, and styles that are in contact in this complex, (non)-melting-pot society. On a given day, in a variety of contexts, it is quite possible to hear various dialects of English and Spanish, as well as French, Polish, Russian, Serbo-Croatian, Arabic, Mandarin, Cantonese, Tagalog, Lao, Vietnamese, Italian, Yiddish, German, Punjabi, Hindi, Urdu, and various indigenous and creole languages of North and Central America. Just take a taxi in any major American city and try and guess the language of your driver. One result of these languages in contact is the emergence of many forms of code switching, usually with English, such as Spanish/English, German/English, Italian/English, Yiddish/English, and Chinese/English. Other combinations are also possible, such as Arabic/French, Spanish/Chinese, and Mayan/Spanish. In addition, various forms of both serious and humorous play occur across these language boundaries, in public spaces such as stores, restaurants, and other workplaces, and in the media, from radio to the internet. Speakers of different languages learn and teach each other on the job. I have observed Croatians and Chinese teaching each other their languages as they work together in a department store, and Chinese, Koreans, and Mexicans doing the same in a grocery store. What is exchanged across language boundaries can include forms of politeness such as greetings, leave-takings, and service formulas, but also playful and mocking vulgarities, made all the more humorous because they are used in the context of language teaching and learning in a public space. Such play across the boundaries of languages is a major expression of the ethnic, cultural, and, of course, linguistic diversity which characterizes the experience of living in the United States today.

France

As in the United States, speech play in France constitutes time out and time off from the serious stuff of life. Also, as in the United States, speech play is a component of French small talk, but there are subtle differences. The French employ elaborate forms of courtesy and politeness, and are careful to respect others by keeping their distance from them—for example, not invading the personal space of strangers or transactional interactants with verbally intrusive remarks. In post offices, banks, medical laboratories, and other public places, painted lines and signs on floors or doors delineate the personal space of each customer/ patron and keep others away.

As in the entire world, French verbal behavior reflects a contrast and tension between tradition and modernity. One aspect of French tradition is a classic elegance and distinction, which is expressed through elaborate everyday rituals of etiquette.[12] Greetings and leave-takings, thank-yous and acknowledgments of thank-yous provide good examples of French politeness formulae. A common greeting uttered on entering a store or office is *bonjour msieudames* 'good day ladies and gentlemen.' Common leave-takings in the same setting are *au revoir msieudames* 'good-bye ladies and gentlemen,' *bonne journée msieudames* 'good day ladies and gentlemen,' *bonne fin de journée* 'good rest of day,' and, typically uttered just before lunch, *bon appétit*. A common *thank you/ you're welcome* formulaic sequence is the following: the buyer says, "*Merci monsieur*" ('thank you sir'), and the seller responds, "*C'est moi qui vous remercie*" ('It is I who thanks you'). These sequences are so formulaic that they resemble such forms of speech play as figures of speech. And they themselves can be played with, as in the *verlan* form *cimer* (*merci*).

While speech play can occur within the framework of formal etiquette, the more formal the setting and the more bourgeois (in the French sense) the interactants, the less exuberant and the more stylized is the speech play (as in the extremely polite speech play that occurs across tables or with waiters in elegant restaurants). At the same time, the conviviality characteristic of French public life is expressed through speech play, though always within careful limits. Examples are similar to those found in the United States, and the differences involve social-interactional detail. Here is a playful postweekend greeting in an elevator:

A: *Comment vas tu?* 'How are you?'
B: *Comme un lundi matin* 'Like a Monday morning.'

And a playful, mock greeting from a waiter to customers he knows personally as they enter a restaurant, pretending they have not reserved a table that they obviously have reserved:

Vous avez reservé? 'Do you have a reservation?'

Again, as in the United States and other complex societies, in France immigration has introduced new and different languages and communicative styles. These are incorporated into verbal practices, providing material for speech play, including code switching and the mocking of languages and styles. The contemporary, young, cool generation sprinkles its discourse with expressions from Arabic, English, *argot*, *verlan*, rap, and hip-hop, in a playful although still controlled (*a la française*) way.

Markets

The setting par excellence for speech play in France is the public market. The tradition of French marketplace speech play began in the Middle Ages and continues through today, incorporating verbal and nonverbal elements from many sources. Here the transactional and the playful meet in the open air. Market cries involve play of many kinds—repetition and parallelism, of sounds and words; loud, aggressive banter; lilting intonations; double entendre and sexual innuendo; interactional license; and verbal dueling. There is a great variety of languages, dialects, and styles of speaking.[13] I end my discussion of speech play in France with a representative selection of speech play in the marketplace. First some very common cries:

Allez. Abricots mures.
'Let's go. Ripe apricots.'
La belle salade, coupée ce matin.
'Beautiful salad, picked this morning.'
Vignt francs la pièce la pastèque.
'Twenty francs the watermelon.'

Comparisons of various kinds are common:

Des prix moins chers que gratuit.
'Prices lower than free.'
Dix francs c'est même pas le prix d'une bouteille de Volvic.
'Ten francs, it's not even the price of a bottle of Volvic (mineral water).'
Meilleurs que mon mari. Deux melons.
'Better than my husband. Two melons.'

Here are parallel constructions:

La belle ail. La belle échalote.
'Beautiful garlic. Beautiful shallot.'

Belles cerises, beaux melons, extra.
'Beautiful cherries, beautiful melons, extra.'
Des affaires, des cadeaux. Du bon du bon.
'Bargains, gifts. It's good, it's good.'

A playful teasing form of economic (il)logic, embedded in a framed dialogue with oneself:

Vous savez pourquoi les gens achètent pas mes cerises? Parce qu'elles sont pas chères.
'Do you know why people do not buy my cherries? Because they are not expensive.'

Puns abound:

Allez cinquante balles dans les shorts. Cinquante balles pour aller aux bals.
'Let's go, fifty francs for shorts. Fifty francs to go to balls.' (The pun is between *balles* [slang for *francs*] and *bals* 'balls, dances').

As does playful verbal dueling:

Seller to passing woman: *Goutte ça chérie.*
'Taste that, dear.'
Male customer: *Moi, il m'appelle pas chérie.*
'Me, he does not call me "dear."'

Finally, a commentary on multiethnic France from a French seller in an African neighborhood market in Paris, where one can buy all sorts of African fruits and vegetables but where he is selling traditional, continental French produce:

Les tomates sont françaises. On mange français aujourd'hui.
'The tomatoes are French. We are eating French today.'

The conviviality of the French market is nicely summed up by a woman to a friend she happened to run into at a Saturday-morning outdoor market:

On dépense nos sous. Même si on n'a pas besoin. Ça ne fait rien.
'We spend our money. Even if we don't need to. It doesn't make any difference.'

Latin America

In addition to my focus on various forms of speech play and verbal art among the Kuna Indians of Panama, in this book I have examined non-indigenous, European- or African-derived communicative forms in Latin America such as play languages, verbal dueling, and song lyrics. In Latin America, rituals and festivals, both indigenous and nonindigenous, and including carnivals and village fiestas, are one of the major settings for speech play and verbal art.

In indigenous curing rites, a magical charm or chant, addressed to representatives of the spirit world, is often the centerpiece of the event. In Kuna magical chants, through a combination of speech play and verbal art the spirits are counseled, cajoled, tricked, and convinced to do the bidding of the performer—calm a high fever, alleviate a headache, or control a dangerous snake.

One of the most ritual of all Kuna traditions are the puberty rites held for young girls. These female initiation rites involve many events, primary among them the ritual cutting of the girl's hair and the performance of long chants to the spirit of a long, sacred flute. In addition, these rites are the only occasion on which the normally sober Kuna drink alcoholic beverages. In fact, the making of corn or sugarcane *chicha*, and the drinking of *chicha* as well as beer and rum, are central and necessary aspects of these rites. Along with the drinking comes much playful and joking behavior, at times quite aggressive.[14]

Nonindigenous Mardi Gras and carnivals often have rituals of reversal as their central, defining features, including both nonverbal and verbal elements. Rituals of reversal are play par excellence. Deviant behavior of all kinds is foregrounded. During carnivals, from Brazil to the Caribbean, men dress as women, whites as Indians and blacks, the young as old, and humans as animals. Performers and participants tease, push, and attack one another and spectators; throw things at people, take things from them, and drag them into the flow of action; and engage in sexual mimicry. Individuals aggressively ask acquaintances as well as strangers for drink and money. A feeling of chaos and license suffuses the scene.[15]

In carnivals in towns of the Panamanian interior, in particular Las Tablas, two processions parade through the streets during carnival evenings. One comes from *calle arriba* 'the street above' and the other comes from *calle abajo* 'the street below,' both singing playful insults aimed at each other. In the ritual of the Congos of the Afro-Panamanians of the Atlantic Coast, in addition to an elaborate dance drama which involves the entire community both spatially and personally, everything that is possible to do backwards is done backwards. People dress as the opposite sex, stand on their heads, smoke cigarettes with the lit part in their mouths, shake their feet instead of their hands, and speak a play language based on semantic reversals.[16] Instead of ¿cuántos años tiene? 'how old are you?' they say ¿cuántos años no tiene en la muerte? 'how many years have you not been dead?'; instead of ven acá 'come here,' they say va pa fuera 'go away'; instead of buenos días 'good morning,' they say buenas noches 'good night.'

On Corpus Christi day in the interior Panamanian town of Los Santos, people wear devil and animal masks and are chased out of morning mass by the priest. They then take to the streets for a day and night of dancing and revelry, yelling, drinking and eating, and joking, often imitating animal shouts and noises. Spectators join in the festivities. Carnivals and similar rituals provide the context for many forms of speech play, which are not necessarily a part of the official ritual, including spoken and song duels, masked dancing, and formulaic and improvised insults.

Town and village patron-saint fiestas are extremely widespread in Latin America. While derived in part from Catholicism, they are often a blending of European, indigenous, and African elements. They are a centuries-old releasing of steam through play, celebrations which are simultaneously religious and antireligious, hegemonic and counterhegemonic, serious, playful, and humorous.[17]

Of the many such fiestas I have observed, I will focus on the joint fiestas of Altar de Maíz and San Martín de la Cruz in the state of Guanajuato, Mexico.[18] These fiestas share features with festivals found throughout Latin America and have unique aspects as well. While the rancho (village) of Altar de Maíz and the city of San Martín de la Cruz are mestizo, many people in these communities consider themselves indigenous, and there is a strong indigenous component to the fiestas, especially to the linking of the two. Older individuals in Altar de Maíz speak Otomí, and Otomí cultural practices continue to exist. A group of Chichimecs live in the neighborhood of Procesión in San Martín de la Cruz; people of all ages in this neighborhood speak Chichimec. The two fiestas are linked in that the communities of Altar de Maíz and San Martín de la Cruz view them as a contemporary manifestation of the alliance between the Otomí and the Chichimecs following the Chichimec wars. Thus they have symbolic as well as historical import. Each of the communities, in its entirety, makes a pilgrimage to the fiesta of the other. The climax of each fiesta is the encuentro 'encounter' between the two communities, a moment in which the two pilgrimages meet, one coming from the center of the community holding the fiesta and the other from the companion community.

The fiesta of Altar de Maíz takes place in December and January; the fiesta of San Martín de la Cruz takes place in August. These fiestas include elements found in many Mexican fiestas. Some of these are sacred and religious, such as all-night vigils with prayers, blessings, and songs in honor of local saints; masses in church; and processions. Others, while not conventionally religious, are official and crucial parts of the fiesta, such as the masked dancing and ritual parade and slaughter of a bull, and the eating of a soup made from the bull and vegetables grown in the community. Still others express aspects of Mexican history, such as the dance drama of a war between Apache Indians and French, no doubt a transformation of the widespread *moros y cristianos* 'Moors and Christians' dance, and symbolizing the conversion of the Indians to Christianity. And others are less official but always present, such as fireworks, food of all kinds, drinking, a rodeo, and social dancing.[19]

Speech play and verbal art can and do occur during all aspects of these fiestas. They are particularly developed and elaborated during the preparations for and breaks in such official and crucial aspects as the processions, the all-night vigils, and the dance dramas, as well as the moments of eating, drinking, social dancing, and relaxation. The verbal and nonverbal play is constant and boisterous. It includes complex puns and allusions to sexual matters, aggressive verbal and nonverbal interactions and dueling, exaggerated imitations of ordinary behavior, comic routines, stylized speech and banter, and much laughter. Symbolic allusions can be complex. During a break in the singing of religious hymns during the all-night vigil of December 30–31, 1997 (a vigil that is part of the fiesta of Altar de Maíz), one of the young male musicians who is by now quite drunk with laced *atole* looks at his mother—seated, wrapped in a serape, sleeping—and says, in Spanish, "She's like the sleeping volcano." There is much laughter. Referring to the sleeping volcano of Mexico, called by its Nahuatl name *iztac sihuatl*, this remark alludes to the great deal of history and symbolism associated with Mexico's indigenous legacy, much a part of these people and this event. In addition, the mother is indeed like a volcano, powerful, protective, and explosive. Some moments before, one of her grandsons had asked her permission to sleep on her lap, and a few minutes later her drunken son suddenly went to sleep on her lap, then got up and began playing his guitar again. This woman and the set of events surrounding her is at the intersection of the old and new, traditional and modern, serious and playful which are so key to this fiesta. There is also much joking about the food and drink, the spiciness of the former and the inebriating effects of the latter, all alluding to sexuality and especially masculine sexual prowess.

The fiestas of Altar de Maíz and San Martín de la Cruz, like all Latin

American rituals and festivals, reflect in many ways the heart and soul of Latin America, in its historic and prehistoric, ethnic, religious, and sociocultural complexity. These rituals and festivals are, for both natives and outsiders—from tourists to members of the diaspora to urban centers and the north, many of whom come back at festival time—models of and models for behavior and conceptualization.[20] They are ethnic identity markers, expressions of community solidarity, reflections of nation-state–Indian relations, and playings out of the tension between the official Catholic religion and local and popular religious practices. As Latin America becomes more and more industrialized, globalized, neoliberalized, free-marketized, and touristed, rituals and fiestas become more and more the sites for group and individual expressions of opposition and resistance to all this as well as adherence to more traditional, sometimes ancient, and yet still evolving forms of symbolism and play.

The Kuna

The Kuna Indians of Panama are a traditional South American tropical-forest indigenous society living on the edge of modern civilization. Aspects of Kuna speech play and verbal art that I have presented in this book include play languages, humorous riddles and lexical neologisms, grammatical and sociolinguistic stretching and manipulation, repetition and parallelism, figurative language and metaphor, trickster tales, and the language of magic and ritual. These are not unique to the Kuna, but they enter into a constellation of speaking practices that focus on speech play and verbal art, including humor in a central way, which is unique.

Kuna humor, like verbal art, is intimately related to play. Joking and humor are notoriously difficult to translate from one language and culture to another, but I hope here to provide some flavor of the Kuna variety. The Kuna do not have jokes of the type found in the European tradition, jokes ending in a clearly marked punch line that actualizes a setup. Nor do they have interactional jokes in which the punch line victimizes the receiver-respondent of the joke. At the same time, Kuna life is punctuated by a great deal of verbal humor and joking. Laughter is omnipresent.

One common form of playful humor involves play names or nicknames. Many animals have play names, and they are usually based on physical characteristics of the animal. Play names are akin to the many metaphors used in quite serious and ritual contexts. They can be used by themselves, as a humorous focal point, in conversations whose sole purpose is recreation and amusement. They are also used in stories about animals, in order to talk about the characters in the story and embellish the humorous aspects of the performance. And they can be used in riddles (see Chapter 3 for a discussion of Kuna riddles). Play names are also used for humans. Typically these are based on animals, thus relating the human and animal worlds. Examples are *kelu* 'jack,' used for an albino businessman who, like this Caribbean fish, is slippery, white, and fat, and *ia korki* 'Uncle pelican,' who looks and acts like a pelican and lives in a house built by the water on the rocks.[21] Finally, play names are used for outsiders—Kuna from other villages, Panamanian officials, Peace Corps volunteers, and anthropologists. Among the Kuna themselves, with outsiders, and in animal stories, play names are part of the teasing, bantering, and riddling interactions of which the Kuna are forever fond.

Another area of verbal humor is imitation and mimicry. Everyday verbal imitations are usually very brief and draw on the stereotypical verbal features of a particular social role or genre. Thus a Kuna man, passing through the relatively empty gathering house during the daytime, might stop in front of the empty hammock of a village chief and for a few seconds imitate the chanting of chiefs, using the very characteristic melodic shape of this chanting and its unique lexical, phonological, morphological, and syntactic features—in particular, the elements used to frame lines and verses. Or a man or woman might sit on a bench and mimic a couple of lines of a magical, curing chant, including the characteristic pose which involves a closed hand raised to the face. Foreigners are also the butt of fleeting imitations. Black Colombian sailors who trade with the Kuna at times speak some Kuna. The Kuna enjoy imitating their accent.[22]

A third area of everyday play, joking, and humor is the verbal put-on or trick, called *yartakke* in Kuna. Verbal tricking within everyday interaction is extremely common among the Kuna. It often occurs between close friends and family members; it can also be used with outsiders. There are many possible topics for verbal put-ons, common among them hunger, sickness, death, physical deformity, and sexual relations and adventures. Matters related to economic relations are also common. Here are a few examples:

A woman tells a visitor, "My child is a dwarf. He can't grow."
A woman returns a gourd to a friend which she had borrowed in order to carry some food. The lender says to the borrower, "I lent you a new gourd and you returned an old one."
A man enters a friend's house to visit him; a member of the friend's family tells the man, "Your friend has died."
A woman makes a lot of noise to imitate an animal, thus frightening a neighbor who lives next door.[23]

Humor is not compartmentalized by the Kuna, restricted to particular specific or marginal occasions and places. Rather, play and joking turn up everywhere, often side by side and even within the most serious forms of speech and action. From the most everyday and passing joke to the full-fledged performance of a trickster tale, humor is not just time out and time off from the serious stuff of life. Its close association with misfortune and disaster; its actualization of, reflection of, exaggeration of, and commentary on social and cultural realities; and its playing around with ritual matters flirt with danger and no doubt heighten its appeal. In many ways play and humor are at the heart of what it means to be Kuna.

Speech play and verbal art are for the Kuna acts of identity and even resistance.[24] Rather than adapt European poetic principles such as rhyme schemes or metric patterns, or genres such as poems or jokes, the Kuna have maintained their own indigenous discourse principles and patterns. At the same time, with increasing migration to Panama City, education, and literacy in Spanish, dramatic changes in Kuna discourse patterning are beginning to occur.[25] There is thus a balance and tension between tradition and change, as pressures from beyond the Kuna world impinge more and more on the Kuna, and are reflected in their discourse, including their speech play and verbal art.

The Kuna ideology of speaking practices in general, and speech play and verbal art in particular, reflects the Kuna's geographical location in the heart of the Americas, at the intersection of North and South America. The Kuna share with indigenous North Americans a ritualized respect for language, a love of the word but a care for its use, and the use of silence when necessary.[26] At the same time, the Kuna love exuberant talk, and talk means play with and about language, for humorous as well as aesthetic purposes. This feature is shared with lowland South American indigenous groups.[27] The Kuna, like most indigenous groups in the Americas, are aware and proud of the distinctiveness of their speaking practices, especially in contrast to the verbal practices of the increasingly dominant, surrounding nonindigenous populations. The Kuna believe that their speech play and verbal art—like and in some ways related to their tropical-forest ecology, considered by the Kuna to be essential to their survival—are what make them Kuna, and they recognize that they are in a struggle to maintain them.

The Balinese

For the Balinese, speech play and verbal art are the constitutive elements of what an astute observer of Bali has called "subversive play."[28] Forms of Balinese speech play that I have described here include puns, verbal duels, riddles, and play languages. Balinese verbal as well as visual art is duly famous, found ritually in shadow-puppet performances, masked dances, and dance dramas. In all of these, serious stories told in ancient languages are interspersed with incredibly clownish behaviors. Perhaps the most striking and characteristic form of play in Bali is the dialogic verbal duel, characteristic of a range of contexts from everyday banter to the performances of clowns in dramatic performances. In the verbal duel, life copies art and art copies life, as one finds *panasars* 'humorous clowns' on both the stage and in the street.

Verbal dueling which projects paradigms syntagmatically is classic clown behavior, picked up by such vaudeville and film comedians as the Marx brothers, as well as such avant-garde playwrights as Samuel Beckett and Eugene Ionesco. That we find Marx brothers–like and Beckett-like verbal routines on the streets, stages, and screens of Bali should be interesting in and of itself. Its broader significance in terms of Balinese social and cultural life, however, remains to be explored. The punful, tricksterlike comebacks of Bali are different from anything I know of elsewhere. They often involve the multilingualism and polyglossia of relations and interactions among Balinese speech levels, Balinese versus Indonesian, and even Balinese versus Indonesian versus English.

To peel away a bit of what is going on here we can start with the observations of Mikhail Bakhtin, who points out that heteroglossia is a basic underpinning of play.[29] Bali provides us with a great example. There is plenty of heteroglossia in Bali; and the similarities in the phonologies and morphologies of the languages and speech levels allow for many homonyms and near homonyms across the sociolinguistic system—which are also coupled with a remarkable ability for hearing, interpreting, and making similarities occur. But homonyms in themselves are not puns: they must be *actualized* as puns and comebacks. It is not obvious or predictable that Balinese heteroglossia should lead to the particular forms of speech play found in Bali, or that they should be omnipresent in so many realms of Balinese verbal life. Features that I would find particularly hard to predict are the exuberance of comeback behavior, given that such behavior is somewhat aggressive; the frequent reversal of and play with speech levels associated with this comeback behavior, given that these levels are so basic to Balinese culture and society; and the trickster behavior located in the everyday rituals of greetings, leave-takings, and ordinary requests. And all of this in a place so focused on decorum and etiquette, in both ideology and practice.

By drawing attention to Balinese speech play and humor, I hope to add them to the list of images of Bali so nicely delineated by Adrian Vickers.[30] These include Bali as a tropical paradise, Bali as a land of beautiful people (especially women), Bali as an expression of artistic grace and elegance, and Bali as the place of fabulous rituals such as cremations. Of course, the images discussed by Vickers are those held by outsiders, or imposed on Bali by outsiders. But play and humor, especially of the type I have discussed here, are intimately related to and expressed through native language and speech, and are thus often unappreciated by or even unperceived by outsiders. Furthermore, and more to the point, the image of the Balinese as playful and humorous is mainly one the Balinese hold of themselves. In fact, it is an ethnic identity marker, indeed an act of identity, imagined and constructed and enacted through everyday verbal interactions and dramatic performances.[31] It contrasts with the constructed ethnic identities of significant others, for example, the Javanese—whose culture shares many traits with the Balinese and yet who are felt and constructed by the Balinese as quite different, especially in their expressive behavior—and, increasingly, foreign visitors and tourists from many places.

Balinese speech play can also be interpreted as subversive, a weapon against the many hegemonic and dominant invaders Bali has had to contend with over the years: the Dutch, the Japanese, the Javanese, and now the tourists, including Americans, Europeans, Japanese, and Australians.[32] Just as Balinese clowns and clownish behavior are consciously and unconsciously critical of the ancient Balinese social order, including its religious and caste system, they are explicitly and implicitly critical of the contemporary social order, that of Bali, Indonesia, and the world.

Those scholars who have paid attention to Balinese speech play offer different interpretations and perspectives. Gregory Bateson and Margaret Mead note the play with speech levels in theatrical performances; they state that the levels continually provide material for joking and mockery, either to be exaggerated and embroidered upon or to be reversed. They provide a psychological interpretation, which is not surprising given their perspective, arguing that the speech levels are a source of continual anxiety and thus emerge as a source of continual amusement in the play and humor of drama.[33] Richard Wallis also discusses the purposeful, comic use of play with, and the reversal of, speech levels; he offers both a sociolinguistic and symbolic perspective, depicting the existence and constant use of different languages and speech levels in Bali as part of "the Balinese preference for a multiple conceptualization of the world."[34] Mark Hobart and Mary Zurbuchen study the importance of sound associations—including puns and comebacks—in the formation of the Balinese symbolic system, from the most ritual to the most everyday symbols.[35] Ron Jenkins views humor and play in Bali as "subversive," in that it is a way of countering outside influences such as tourism while maintaining the social order.[36]

The study of Balinese speech play leads us to both humor and aesthetics. The two are related. The speech play of everyday interactions is taken further in the aesthetics of drama, while at the same time drama provides and reinforces frames for everyday interactions. Speech play in Bali provides implicit and explicit native metacommentary—in the form of the praxis of everyday life and artistic performances—on Balinese systems and structure, linguistic, sociolinguistic, and cultural. Of particular interest in this regard is the Balinese people's constant awareness of speech levels and associated semantic sets, which is reflected in their puns and comebacks, and, in fact, often underlies the complexity of these speech acts. The ritual and sociological tension involved in Balinese speech levels is reflected in the playful and fleetingly (as well as flirtingly) insulting misuse of levels as well as their often mixed use in everyday speech.

Balinese speech play often has the effect of being illogical, absurd, and strange—characteristics that are appreciated in Balinese verbal art and aesthetics more generally. Play explores and indeed flirts with the boundaries of the socially and culturally possible and appropriate; for this reason it is often felt to be simultaneously disjunctive and cohesive, humorous, serious, and aesthetically pleasing.

It seems appropriate to stress here the danger always inherent in speech play. The more that play flirts with danger—involving social, cultural, linguistic, and interactional boundaries and possibilities of all kinds—the funnier it gets. But the danger—social, cultural, linguistic, and interactional—is ever present.[37] It also teaches us that play and joking are often about social boundaries (us versus them), of which there are plenty in Bali: caste, class, occupation, ethnicity (including Balinese versus Javanese), and nation (including Bali versus Java, Indonesia, and other countries). Bali provides us with an excellent illustration of speech play as a cultural focus. In other words, Bali teaches us just how serious play can be.

Some Final Thoughts

As we enter the twenty-first century, there are clearly contrasts, contradictions, and conflicts between a global economy dominated by monolithic capitalism and expressed through English and a few other major world languages (referentially and transactionally oriented and focused), and the many local, minority, marginal, dominated, and subaltern groups struggling to maintain their social identity and cultural integrity. For the former, the hegemonic, speech play and verbal art are time out and time off from the serious stuff of life—or, as I have argued for the United States and feel is true for Western, industrialized society more generally, grease and oil for referential transactions. For the latter, the nonhegemonic, and for each in their own and very, very different and distinct ways, speech play and verbal art can be and often are important vehicles of expression of who they are and of counterhegemonic resistance.

It is particularly valuable to examine the cases of local, minority, marginal, and especially subordinate and subaltern groups, cultures, and languages—Native Americans, Jews, Balinese, Corsicans, Alpine as well as southern Italians, Caribbean Creoles, African Americans, and Hispanics, among many others. In these languages and cultures, the voices of the weak become critical and vibrant voices, often in a humorous vein, emerging in jokes and other forms of speech play and verbal art. These voices are expressed, represented, and juxtaposed to those of their significant Others—those that dominate, oppress, or persecute them— as well as the homogenizing voice of the globalized, market-oriented world more generally. They mock and are mocked, and ultimately are weapons of the weak against the strong.[38] They constitute the quintessential and exuberant expression of just who people are. As a Kuna woman once said to me concerning talk, play, and humor among the Kuna: "The Kuna place is not a quiet place. It is a talking place and a laughing place."[39] And as a man in Tobago remarked to me about his language, Tobago creole: "Any word take a word you can twist it and turn anyhow, the dialect (creole) is concerned. You could say anything and you could make fun outa everything, almost everything."[40] In this sense, jokes in particular and speech play and verbal art more generally play a significant role in the invention, the imagination, and the construction of selves and communities, and in the political economy and ideology of language use.[41]

There are many ways to interpret and imagine the place of speech play and verbal art in the world today, ways which articulate with contemporary theoretical perspectives and empirical studies in anthropology, political science, sociology, linguistics, and literary criticism. Speech play and verbal art emerge out of the heteroglossic and cultural diversity of the worlds we live in, out of the intertextual gaps that occur when languages, styles, genres, and cultures are in contact. They contribute to the imagined community and the invention of tradition, and they create and construct social and cultural identity. They express the political unconscious—but also the social, cultural, linguistic, individual, and political unconscious and conscious of real people in real situations. They are forms of cultural resistance, ways minority groups deal with majority groups, and weapons of the weak as well as of the strong.[42]

Notice that I am claiming that one possible function of speech play and verbal art in communities around the world is counterhegemony and resistance to domination. And this is no doubt the case. But I do not want to overstress this.[43] Speech play and verbal art are also expressions of social, cultural, and personal identity and consciousness, not necessarily always including resistance to a particular power structure, and they are appreciated for the sheer pleasure and creativity of play and art for their own sake.

A tradition of scholarship from Saussure through Sapir and Whorf to Bakhtin and Derrida focuses on differences, both cultural and linguistic, and especially their relationship. When there is difference there is often a power differential. And when difference is combined with a power differential, this combination is reflected in and expressed through speech play and verbal art.[44] Speech play and verbal art, emerging out of and celebrating heteroglossic hybridities and power differentials, reflect and introduce discrepancies and contradictions. Furthermore, they challenge the neatness of many oppositions regarding language, culture, society, and literature that scholars often find convenient—oral/literate; pure/mixed; high, elite/low, popular; traditional/avant-garde; grammatical/ungrammatical; endangered/thriving; powerful/powerless; and even hegemonic/counterhegemonic.

Under the rubric of speech play and verbal art I have examined a large variety of phenomena. I have listed them, catalogued them, and illustrated them with many examples from various parts of the world. This is necessary in order to show the range of possibilities of speech play and verbal art, the relations between and among them, and their significance. In keeping with a long tradition of linguistic anthropology, I hold that it is critical for culture and society, including identity, political economy, and ideology, to be studied in relation to language and language use, where they are reflected, expressed, and created. To this I would add that speech play and verbal art should be seen as a central and most significant and revealing aspect of the language-culture-society nexus.

Another way to view this is in terms of the concept of linguistic creativity, a topic of interest to linguists from ancient times to the present, as well as to literary scholars. Linguistic creativity is not limited to grammar as a set of formal rules, however complicated, but rather emerges in language use—in particular, in speech play and verbal art and their intersection. This raises the questions of boundaries. Where does grammar end and discourse begin? What is serious discourse and what is playful and aesthetic discourse? These boundaries themselves are not fixed but rather are constructed by speakers and performers, and emerge in the context of language use.

Every group, dominant or dominated, hegemonic or subaltern, major or minor, majority or minority, operates according to a set of ideologies and tropes, sometimes explicitly articulated, sometimes implicit—

about culture, society, politics, ethnicity, economics, language, personality, literature, and their interrelationships. According to the sociolinguistic, ethnographic, and discourse-centered approach I advocate and illustrate in this book, everyday speaking practices reflect, express, contribute to, create, re-create, and transmit these ideologies and tropes. I hope to have shown, theoretically, methodologically, and especially by means of explicit cases, that among these speaking practices speech play and verbal art occupy a prominent place.

Notes

Chapter One. Introduction

1. Sapir 1915 (reprinted in Mandelbaum 1963: 181).
2. Sapir 1921: 38.
3. *Webster's third new international dictionary of the English language, unabridged*, s.v. "play."
4. See Huizinga 1955: 28–46.
5. See Bateson 1972; Goffman 1974.
6. See Hymes 1974; Jakobson 1971.
7. I borrow and expand on this very useful concept of Erving Goffman (1983).
8. See Da Matta 1991.
9. See Slater 1982.
10. See Sherzer 1983, 1990.
11. See Vickers 1989.
12. See especially Apte 1985; Attardo 1994; K. H. Basso 1979; P. Berger 1997; Bruner, Jolly, and Sylva 1976; Caillois 1961; Crystal 1998; Durant and Miller 1988; Freud 1905; Garvey 1977; Huizinga 1955; Kirshenblatt-Gimblett 1976; Millar 1968; Nachmanovitch 1990; Norrick 1993; Palmer 1994; Piaget 1951; Piddington 1963; Yaguello 1998. Lewis Carroll's *Alice in Wonderland* (1951), though technically a novel, is a classic philosophical essay on speech play.
13. See Bauman 1977b; Bauman and Sherzer 1989; Finnegan 1992; Sherzer 1990.
14. See Hymes 1981; Sammons and Sherzer 2000; Sherzer and Urban 1986; Sherzer and Woodbury 1987; Tedlock 1983.
15. See Hill 1993.
16. See Bakhtin 1981; Briggs and Bauman 1992.

Chapter Two. The Grammar of Play and the Play of Grammar

1. Jakobson 1960, 1968.
2. Peirce 1932.
3. This relationship between the expression of size, both augmentative

and diminutive, and affective sociolinguistic expression—with augmentative being derogatory or pejorative and diminutive being endearing—is rather widespread in language. Examples include the French request *faites-moi une petite signature* 'make a little signature for me' (= please sign this) and certain Spanish dialects' use of diminutives for affection and intimacy, as in ¿*Cómo estás Joelito?* 'How are you (little) Joel?'

4. Notice that glottalization is also involved in the first two examples. These examples are from Sapir 1911: 640.

5. It is interesting that Sapir refers to this phenomenon as "consonantal play," using the very term (*play*) which is the subject of this book. See Chapter 1 and Sapir 1915 (reprinted in Mandelbaum 1963: 181).

6. Jakobson and Waugh (1979) discuss sound symbolism and iconicity more generally. See also Feld 1982, which deals with sound symbolism and other forms of speech play and verbal art among the New Guinea Kaluli. Nuckolls 1996 deals with sound symbolism among the Ecuadorian Quechua. Hinton, Nichols, and Ohala 1994 is a useful collection of papers dealing with sound symbolism.

7. Sherzer 1987.

8. "El rey," a song written by José Alfredo Jimenez.

9. My examples are from my own research on the Milpa Alta dialect of Nahuatl and from one of the many grammatical descriptions of Nahuatl, that of Stanley Newman (1967).

10. These last two examples are from "The Agouti story," performed by Chief Muristo Pérez. See Sherzer 1990.

11. From "The Agouti story."

12. These last two examples are from "The Turtle and Monkey story," performed by Chief Nipakkinya. See Sherzer 1997.

13. Jakobson 1968.

14. Useful literature on reduplication includes Jakobson and Waugh 1979; Moravcsik 1992; Sapir 1921; and Thun 1963.

Chapter Three. Forms of Speech Play in Context

1. See Bagemihl 1989; McCarthy 1986; Sherzer 1982; Yip 1982.

2. See Calvet 1994: 281–285.

3. An ancient European rhetorical tradition of pun making goes by the name of *paranomasia*. Bombaugh 1961; Fontanier 1968; Lausberg 1960.

4. Sacks 1973; Sherzer 1978b.

5. Observed in conversation.

6. National Public Radio, *Morning Edition*, November 14, 1997.

7. *Monkey Business*.

8. Piddington 1963.

9. Mahood 1957.

10. *Julius Caesar*, act 1, scene 1.

11. *Romeo and Juliet*, act 3, scene 1.

12. *Duck Soup*.

13. Observed in conversation.

14. National Public Radio, *Morning Edition*, August 23, 1998.

15. Freud 1905 (1974: 49).

16. Observed in conversation.

17. *Hamlet*, act 2, scene 2.

18. Observed in conversation. See discussion of Balinese puns below for more examples of bilingual puns.

19. Sacks 1973.

20. These three were observed in conversation.

21. TV news, Channel 24, Austin, September 22, 1998.

22. TV talk show, January 22, 1998.

23. National Public Radio, *Morning Edition*, October 1, 1998.

24. *CNN Headline News*, June 29, 1998.

25. National Public Radio, *Living on Earth*, August 24, 2000.

26. KUT Austin, *Passport to Texas*, January 6, 1997.

27. National Public Radio, *Morning Edition*, February 9, 2000.

28. Observed in conversation.

29. In the sense of Goffman 1974.

30. Notice the similarities of this example to some of the Balinese examples discussed below.

31. National Public Radio, *Weekend Edition*, January 24, 1998.

32. Among the African Nupe, a society that takes a very negative view toward obscenity, puns are used to tone down obscene allusions. See Nadel 1954.

33. Philips 1985: 321. See also Philips 1975.

34. See Sherzer 1993.

35. Freud 1905.

36. The literature on jokes is enormous. Freud 1905 is, of course, basic. For the linguistic structure of jokes, see Chiaro 1992; Hockett 1973; Wilson 1979.

37. This is also an example of a joke across social boundaries, an issue to be discussed below.

38. Bauman 1977a; Sanches and Kirshenblatt-Gimblett 1976.

39. This joke, like many of the jokes discussed here, is also a joke across social boundaries.

40. Jameson 1981.

41. Draitser 1998.

42. Reported by Dundes 1973: 620.

43. In the sense of Goffman 1974.

44. In the sense of Hill 1993.

45. National Public Radio, *Morning Edition*, September 19, 1998.

46. See Nelson 1999: 373–378.

47. See Davies, 1990, 1998.

48. Douglas 1968; Limón 1978, 1982.

49. See Anderson 1983; Bakhtin 1981; Gal 1989; Scott 1985.

50. The classic reference work on the dirty joke is Legman 1968. See also Sacks 1974.

51. It is interesting in this regard to note that Max Weinreich, in his mon-

umental *History of the Yiddish Language* (1980) devotes considerable space to Jewish humor, exemplified with Jewish jokes. See also A. Berger 1997 and P. L. Berger 1997: Chapter 6.

52. There are many versions of this riddle joke. See Epstein 1969 and Ginzberg 1925.

53. This and most of the Jewish jokes here were told by Esther Eilberg on April 27, 1998.

54. For a related joking approach to significant others, see the "portraits of 'The Whiteman': Apache jokes" reported on in K. H. Basso 1979.

55. Sacks 1974.

56. This last joke was told by Esther Eilberg on April 27, 1998.

57. Goffman 1974: 87. Brackman (1967) offers a somewhat popular account of put-ons.

58. K. H. Basso 1979.

59. Howe and Sherzer 1986. See also E. Basso 1987.

60. Bright 1993; Erdoes and Ortiz 1998.

61. See Geertz 1973 for the notions of *models of* and *models for.*

62. Performed by Chief Muristo Pérez of the Kuna village of Mulatuppu on April 21, 1970 (Sherzer 1990: Chapter 7).

63. Gossen 1974: 114. And from Akan (in Ghana):

When the cockroach falls, it either lands or upturns.
If two set a hunting trap, it takes two to check it.
The mature dog cannot be called a puppy.

—Yankah 1986

64. Personal observations.

65. Personal observation, January 30, 1998.

66. Personal observation, January 5, 2001.

67. Moncef Lahlou, conversation with author, June 1995.

68. Hardesty 1977.

69. Personal observation, April 24, 1994.

70. Personal observation, October 3, 1994.

71. Gossen 1976.

72. In many African societies proverbs are prominent in formal aspects of social life, such as court procedures. In these contexts they are overtly framed and highly noticeable. Arewa and Dundes 1964; Messenger 1959; Yankah 1986.

73. The remainder of the examples in this section are either from personal observation or were collected by my students during the last twenty years.

74. Similarly enigmatic, from Bantu:

Question: Going I found it, returning I found it not.
Answer: Dew.

—Beuchat 1957

In Madagascar riddles often consist of an elaborate metaphorical question and an answer that may be only one word:

Question: Perfume from the forest.
Answer: Ginger.

—Haring 1992: 39

Notice the similarity between these riddles, in form and content, and riddles from both Africa and Oceania. Madagascar is geographically and culturally close to Africa, but linguistically related to the languages of Oceania.
75. Again from Madagascar:

Question: Old man leaning on the wall.
Answer: Boiled rice (because it sticks to the sides of the pot).

—Haring 1992: 42

76. National Public Radio, *Morning Edition*, February 14, 1998.
77. Riddles are extremely widespread in Africa, where riddles and proverbs are closely associated. They are a form of entertainment and instruction for both children and adults. They often become public contests in which one individual challenges another to provide an answer.
In Madagascar, riddling constitutes a small-scale model for a dialogic pattern that pervades much of Malagasy verbal art. In addition, there exists in certain parts of Madagascar a rather unique double riddle called the *safidy* 'choice,' which consists of two riddles combined. The respondent must give the correct interpretation of both parts and choose between them:

Question: Which do you prefer, little eyes in the rocks or big eyes in the grass?
Answer (one of several possible): I prefer the first, which is an ox going to pasture, while the second is a snake stealing chickens.

—Haring 1992: 34–62

78. Abrahams 1983: 167.
79. Reily 1998: 307. I follow Reily's transcription of the local Portuguese.
80. Sherzer 1993.
81. Abrahams 1962; Dundes, Leach, and Özkök 1972; Gossen 1976; Herndon and McLeod 1980; Labov 1972; McDowell 1985; Pagliai 2000; Solomon 1994.
82. Labov 1972: 346, 347, 349.
83. Crook 1998; Gradante 1991; Reily 1998; R. R. Smith 1998.
84. Gradante 1991: 648. I follow Gradante's transcription of the local Spanish.
85. Gradante 1991: 707, 708, 709.

Chapter Four. From Speech Play to Verbal Art

1. Particularly useful treatments of the relationship between linguistics and literature, in the guise of introductory textbooks, are Fabb 1977 and Traugott and Pratt 1980.

2. Bergerson 1973; Bombaugh 1961; Espy 1971; Wells 1963.

3. See Bergerson 1973: 82–90.

4. Bergerson 1973: ix.

5. See Bergerson 1973: 40–81.

6. Bombaugh 1961: 43.

7. Wells 1963: 17.

8. Hymes 1981; Sherzer and Woodbury 1987; Tedlock 1983.

9. Legman 1974.

10. Legman 1974: jacket.

11. See Chapter 3 for a discussion of verbal dueling.

12. I use the names given in the Western tradition. See Corbett 1971. See also Crystal 1997 and Yaguello 1998, who provides an interesting way to classify figures of speech.

13. Psalm 29.

14. Molière, *L'Avare*.

15. John F. Kennedy, inaugural address, January 20, 1961.

16. Jakobson 1971: 578–579; Kiparsky 1973.

17. Chomsky 1965; Ross 1972.

18. See Ross 1972.

19. Thomas 1971: 114.

20. Note that earlier in this chapter, in an example of graffiti, we saw that the word *dollars* can also become an expression of time in this same context.

21. See Crystal 1997: 72.

22. Cummings 1940: 29. This poem is discussed in greater detail below in this chapter.

23. Carroll 1951: 133.

24. The translation is by Frank L. Warrin, in Gardner 1960: 193.

25. Thomas 1971: 88.

26. Neruda 1964.

27. Thomas 1971: 77.

28. From the song "Dos corazones" by Jorge Riojas, on the compact disk *El amor es así*, Ontop Records, OT 9059.

29. Gradante 1991: 648.

30. Sapir 1921: 228.

31. Sapir 1921: 71.

32. See Gayton and Newman 1940 (reprinted as "Linguistic aspects of Yokuts style" in Hymes 1964: 372–377); Friedrich 1979; 1986; Sherzer 1987; 1989.

33. Sherzer 1989.

34. These examples are from "The Agouti story," performed by Chief Muristo Pérez. See Sherzer 1990.

35. From "The report of a curing specialist," performed by Olowikti-nappi. See Sherzer 1990.

36. From "The Agouti story." See also Chapter 3.

37. From "The way of the snake," performed by Pranki Pilos. See Sherzer 1990.

38. From "A counsel to a new chief," performed by Chief Muristo Pérez. See Sherzer 1990.

39. For an excellent description of this phenomenon, see Janda and Morgan 1988.

40. Germaine Montero, *"Lament on the death of a bullfighter," and other poems and songs of Federico García Lorca*, Vanguard Records, VRS 9055.

41. Lakoff and Johnson 1980.

42. See Bright 1990.

43. Sapir 1932: 217–219; Kluckhohn and Leighton 1962: 98; Rushforth 1991. I am also grateful for personal communications with Anthony Webster on this topic.

44. Sherzer 1978a.

45. Bakhtin 1981.

46. See Weeda 1992.

47. Sherzer 1988, Jean 2000.

48. This song is an excellent illustration of the interplay between grammatical and sociolinguistic stretching, syntactic and semantic parallelism, and metaphor that is so characteristic of both oral and written poetry around the world. It will be discussed below.

49. From a performance by the well-known and popular puppeteer I. Wayan Wija, in June 1985.

50. Heller 1988.

51. Hill 1993.

52. El Zol, Miami.

53. Hot KTFM, San Antonio.

54. Zepeda 1995: 15.

55. Paredes 1991: 26–27; originally published in a 1939 high-school yearbook.

56. Alurista 1971: 1–2.

57. Delgado 1969: 20.

58. Written by Augie Meyers and performed by the Texas Tornados, *Texas Tornados*, Reprise Records 4-26251.

59. Gómez-Peña 1996: 190.

60. Anzaldúa 1987: 77.

61. Anzaldúa 1987: 81–82.

62. Anzaldúa 1987: preface, 2.

63. Jones and Neal 1968: 299.

64. Jones and Neal 1968: 255.

65. See Levine 1977; Potter 1995; Smitherman 1977, 1994.

66. Stratton and Wozencraft 1998: 52.

67. Stratton and Wozencraft 1998: 158.

68. Shakur, "Me against the world," www.members.tripod.com/~Lib-byBo/meagainsttheworld.html. This is just one of several transcriptions of this song one can find on the internet.

69. Opie and Opie 1959: 24.

70. Withers 1948: 193.

71. Jakobson 1960, 1966, 1968. Johnstone 1994 is a useful collection of papers dealing with repetition and parallelism.

72. I observed and recorded these and all other examples of everyday speech provided in this book in actual, natural settings.

73. March 3, 1998.

74. April 3, 1998.

75. Wyman 1970: 26.

76. Léon-Portilla 1969: 134–135.

77. Tedlock 1985: 80–81.

78. Seeger 1986: 74–75.

79. Seeger 1986: 75.

80. This discussion of "The way of basil" draws on Sherzer 1992.

81. From "The way of basil," performed by Pranki Pilos.

82. Sherzer and Sherzer 1976.

83. Lakoff and Johnson 1980.

84. I am using the term *metaphor* here in a very general sense. Other terms have been also used in this generic sense, for example, *trope* and *symbol*. There is no general agreement here and fashions change. *Trope*, for example, which used to be a generic term for literary scholars, is now most often used to mean metaphors or other figures of speech and even actions, such as silence, which are central to a culture or to a work of art. This usage has become very common in anthropology.

85. K. H. Basso 1967.

86. Brugman 1983.

87. Personal observation. August 8, 1998.

88. Howe 1977; Sherzer 1990: Chapter 4.

89. Kenney 1998.

90. ABC news, February 17, 1999.

91. Jakobson 1960: 363.

92. Levin 1964; Thorne 1965; Traugott and Pratt 1980.

93. Cummings 1940: 29.

94. *Conjunto: Texas-Mexican border music*, Rounder Records 6023.

95. *Jacques Brel: Encore*, Reprise Records 6246.

Chapter Five. Contexts for Speech Play

1. Of course Goffman 1974 is crucial here, as elsewhere.

2. I personally observed each of these. I have been collecting and enjoying such cases for more than fifteen years, and it gives me pleasure to be able to share them with others. They include quite a few from tennis, a game I am very familiar with, in both its game frame and its speech-play frame.

3. This distinction is based on a seminal paper by Erving Goffman (1976).

4. Only certain pairs of individuals can interact this way. Note the similarities to joking relationships in places like Africa. See Radcliffe-Brown 1940.

5. See Ide 1998: Chapter 6.

6. Jefferson 1972.

7. D. Sherzer 1978; D. Sherzer and J. Sherzer 1987.

8. Goffman 1971.

9. Goffman 1971: 81. Goffman probably playfully adopted this phrase from the well-known proverb "Nature abhors a vacuum," an English proverb used by many authors, including, in particular, those in Marxist and thus social-structural and economically oriented circles. I am indebted to Richard Bauman for pointing out to me the proverbial origin of this utterance. See W. G. Smith 1948.

10. The French solve this interactional "problem" within their system of formal politeness by using the word *rebonjour* 'hello again.'

11. Carbaugh 1989; Goffman 1974, 1981; Hymes 1996.

12. Bourdieu 1979.

13. See Lindenfeld 1990. See also Bakhtin (1968: 145–195), who studies Rabelais's observation and use of market cries in medieval France.

14. Sherzer 1983, 1990.

15. Da Matta 1991.

16. These examples are from my own research in 1978. See also Joly 1983; Lipski 1989.

17. Brandes 1988; Ingham 1984; Lavenda 1986; Martínez 1998; Milne 1965.

18. I have changed the names of these places.

19. I observed and participated in the fiesta of Altar de Maíz in December 1997 and January 1998 as well as December 2000 and January 2001, and the fiesta of San Martín de la Cruz in August 1999. My research on Mexican fiestas is in collaboration with Yolanda Lastra and Dina Sherzer.

20. For the concept of *model of* and *model for* see Geertz 1973.

21. The naming of humans after animal traits was common in Native America, and this tradition persists in such places as contemporary Mesoamerica. A noteworthy example is *El Pipila*, a hero of the Mexican war of independence against the Spaniards whose enormous statue towers above the city of Guanajuato. *El Pipila*, a native of the region of Guanajuato, was able to trick the Spaniards into letting him enter their fort and then set it on fire, leading to victory for his forces. Because he had smallpox as a child he was left with a pockmarked face, speckled like a *pipila* 'turkey egg'—hence his name.

22. These brief imitations of foreigners resemble the Apache portraits of "The Whiteman," analyzed by K. H. Basso 1979.

23. See Sherzer 1990: Chapter 7. Kuna everyday verbal tricking is in some ways quite similar to the put-ons described by Philips (1975) for the Warm Springs Indian reservation and other North American Indian communities.

See also Paredes (1977), who analyzes the role of play, humor, and put-ons in native-outsider relations. Howe and Sherzer (1986) analyze the relationship between Kuna put-ons and the narratives told about them, with a focus on Kuna/-outside anthropologist interactions.

24. Le Page and Tabouret-Keller 1985.

25. Sherzer 1994.

26. K. H. Basso 1970; Sherzer 1983.

27. E. B. Basso 1987.

28. Jenkins 1994.

29. Bakhtin 1981.

30. Vickers 1989.

31. See Anderson 1983; Le Page and Tabouret-Keller 1985.

32. I am using *weapon* here in the sense of Scott's "weapons of the weak." See Scott 1985.

33. Bateson and Mead 1942.

34. Wallis 1980: iv.

35. Hobart 1978, 1990; Zurbuchen 1987.

36. Jenkins 1994.

37. K. H. Basso's (1979) description of joking behavior among the Apaches is a wonderful demonstration of the play-danger interaction. See also Howe and Sherzer 1986; Paredes 1977.

38. In the sense of Scott 1985.

39. Cecilia Quijano.

40. Wendel X.

41. In the sense of Lee 1992 and Schieffelin, Woolard, and Kroskrity 1998. See also Paredes 1977, a pioneering and provocative essay.

42. Anderson 1983; Bakhtin 1981; Bhabha 1994; Briggs and Bauman 1992; Camaroff 1985; Hall 1976; Hill 1985; Hobsbawm and Ranger 1983; Jameson 1981; Le Page and Tabouret-Keller 1985; Scott 1985, 1990.

43. See Brown 1996.

44. Bakhtin 1981; Derrida 1970, 1996; Sapir 1921; Schulz 1990; Whorf 1956.

References

Abrahams, Roger D. 1962. Playing the dozens. *Journal of American Folklore* 75: 209–220.

———. 1983. *The man-of-words in the West Indies: Performance and the emergence of creole culture.* Baltimore: Johns Hopkins University Press.

Alurista. 1971. *Floricanto en Aztlán.* Los Angeles: Chicano Cultural Center, University of California, Los Angeles.

Anderson, Benedict. 1983. *Imagined communities: Reflections on the origin and spread of nationalism.* London: Verso.

Anzaldúa, Gloria. 1987. *Borderlands/La frontera: The new mestiza spinsters.* San Francisco: Aunt Lute Books.

Apte, Mahadev L. 1985. *Humor and laughter: An anthropological approach.* Ithaca, N.Y.: Cornell University Press.

Arewa, E. Ojo, and Alan Dundes. 1964. Proverbs and the ethnography of speaking folklore. *American Anthropologist* 66 (6) (Special Publication, *The ethnography of communication,* edited by John J. Gumperz and Dell Hymes): 70–85.

Attardo, Salvatore. 1994. *Linguistic theories of humor.* Berlin: Mouton de Gruyter.

Bagemihl, Bruce. 1989. The crossing constraint and 'backwards languages.' *Natural Language and Linguistic Theory* 7: 481–549.

Bakhtin, Mikhail M. 1968. *Rabelais and his world.* Cambridge, Mass.: MIT Press.

———. 1981. *The dialogic imagination.* Austin: University of Texas Press.

Basso, Ellen B. 1987. *In favor of deceit: A study of tricksters in an Amazonian society.* Tucson: University of Arizona Press.

Basso, Keith H. 1967. Semantic aspects of linguistic acculturation. *American Anthropologist* 69: 471–477.

———. 1970. 'To give up on words': Silence in Western Apache culture. *Southwestern Journal of Anthropology* 26: 213–230.

———. 1979. *Portraits of "the Whiteman": Linguistic play and cultural symbols among the Western Apache.* Cambridge: Cambridge University Press.

Bateson, Gregory. 1972. *Steps to an ecology of mind.* New York: Ballantine Books.

Bateson, Gregory, and Margaret Mead. 1942. *Balinese character: A photographic analysis*. Special Publications of the New York Academy of Sciences, vol. 2. New York: New York Academy of Sciences.

Bauman, Richard. 1977a. Linguistics, anthropology, and verbal art: Toward a unified perspective, with a special discussion of children's folklore. In *Linguistics and Anthropology*, Georgetown University Roundtable on Languages and Linguistics 1977, edited by Muriel Saville-Troike, 13–36. Washington, D.C.: Georgetown University Press.

———. 1977b. *Verbal art as performance*. Rowley, Mass.: Newbury House.

———. 1986. *Story, performance, and event: Contextual studies of oral narrative*. Cambridge: Cambridge University Press.

Bauman, Richard, and Joel Sherzer, eds. 1989. *Explorations in the ethnography of speaking*. Cambridge: Cambridge University Press.

Berger, Arthur A. 1997. *The genius of the Jewish joke*. Northvale, N.J.: Jason Aronson.

Berger, Peter L. 1997. *Redeeming laughter: The comic dimension of human experience*. Hawthorne, N.Y.: Walter de Gruyter.

Bergerson, Howard W. 1973. *Palindromes and anagrams*. New York: Dover.

Beuchat, P. D. 1957. Riddles in Bantu. *African Studies* 16: 133–149.

Bhabha, Homi K. 1994. *The location of culture*. New York: Routledge.

Bombaugh, Charles C. 1961. *Oddities and curiosities of words and literature*. New York: Dover.

Bourdieu, Pierre. 1979. *La distinction: Critique sociale du jugement*. Paris: Editions de Minuit.

Brackman, Jacob. 1967. *The put-on: Modern fooling and modern mistrust*. Chicago: Henry Regnery.

Brandes, Stanley. 1988. *Power and persuasion: Fiestas and social control in rural Mexico*. Philadelphia: University of Pennsylvania Press.

Briggs, Charles, and Richard Bauman. 1992. Genre, intertextuality, and social power. *Journal of Linguistic Anthropology* 2:131–172.

Bright, William. 1984. *American Indian linguistics and literature*. Berlin: Mouton.

———. 1990. "With one lip, with two lips": Parallelism in Nahuatl. *Language* 66: 437–452.

———. 1993. *A coyote reader*. Berkeley: University of California Press.

Brown, Michael F. 1996. On resisting resistance. *American Anthropologist* 98: 729–735.

Brugman, Claudia. 1983. The use of body-part terms as locatives in Chalcatongo Mixtec. In *Survey of California and other Indian languages*, Report no. 4, edited by Alice Schlicter, Wallace L. Chafe, and Leanne Hinton, 235–290. Berkeley: Department of Linguistics, University of California.

Bruner, Jerome, Allison Jolly, and Kathy Sylva, eds. 1976. *Play: Its role in development and evolution*. Harmondsworth, England: Penguin Books.

Caillois, Roger. 1961. *Man, play, and games*. New York: Free Press.

Calvet, Louis-Jean. 1994. *Les voix de la ville: Introduction à la sociolinguistique urbaine*. Paris: Editions Payot et Rivages.

Camaroff, Jean. 1985. *Body of power, spirit of resistance: The culture and history of a South African people.* Chicago: University of Chicago Press.

Carbaugh, Donal. 1989. *Talking American: Cultural discourses on Donahue.* Norwood, N.J.: Ablex.

Carroll, Lewis. [1865] 1951. *Alice in wonderland and other favorites.* Reprint, New York: Washington Square Press.

Chiaro, Delia. 1992. *The language of jokes: Analysing verbal play.* London: Routledge.

Chomsky, Noam. 1965. *Aspects of the theory of syntax.* Cambridge: MIT Press.

Corbett, Edward P. J. 1971. *Classical rhetoric for the modern student.* New York: Oxford University Press.

Crook, Larry. 1998. Brazil: Northeast area. In *The Garland encyclopedia of world music.* Vol. 2, *South America, Mexico, Central America, and the Caribbean,* edited by Dale A. Olsen and Daniel E. Shechy, 323–339. New York: Garland.

Crystal, David. 1997. *The Cambridge encyclopedia of language.* 2d ed. Cambridge: Cambridge University Press.

———. 1998. *Language play.* London: Penguin Books.

cummings, e. e. 1940. *Fifty poems.* New York: Grosset and Dunlap.

Da Matta, Roberto. 1991. *Carnivals, rogues, and heroes: An interpretation of the Brazilian dilemma.* Notre Dame, Ind.: University of Notre Dame Press.

Davies, Christie. 1990. *Ethnic humor around the world: A comparative analysis.* Bloomington: Indiana University Press.

———. 1998. *Jokes and their relation to society.* Berlin: Mouton de Gruyter.

Delgado, Abelardo. 1969. *Chicano: Twenty-five pieces of a Chicano mind.* Denver: Barrio Publications.

Derrida, Jacques. 1970. Structure, sign, and play in the discourse of the human sciences. In *The languages of criticism and the sciences of man: The structuralist controversy,* edited by Richard Macksey and Eugenio Donato, 247–265. Baltimore: Johns Hopkins Press.

———. 1996. *Monolinguisme de l'autre, ou la prothèse d'origine.* Paris: Galilee.

Douglas, Mary. 1968. Jokes. *Man* 3: 361–376.

Draitser, Emil A. 1998. Folk humor of post-Soviet Russia: A survey. Paper presented at 1998 annual meeting of International Society for Humor Studies.

Dundes, Alan, ed. 1973. *Mother wit from the laughing barrel: Readings in the interpretation of Afro-American folklore.* Englewood Cliffs, N.J.: Prentice-Hall.

Dundes, Alan, Jerry W. Leach, and Bora Özkök. 1972. The strategy of Turkish boys' verbal dueling rhymes. In *Directions in sociolinguistics: The ethnography of communication,* edited by John J. Gumperz and Dell Hymes, 130–160. New York: Holt, Rinehart and Winston.

Durant, John, and Jonathan Miller. 1988. *Laughing matters: A serious look at humor.* Essex, England: Longman.

Epstein, Isidore, ed. 1969. *Hebrew-English edition of the Babylonian Talmud, Sanhedrin*. London: Soncino Press.

Erdoes, Richard, and Alfonso Ortiz, eds. 1998. *American Indian trickster tales*. New York: Viking.

Espy, Willard R. 1971. *The game of words*. New York: Grosset and Dunlap.

Fabb, Nigel. 1997. *Linguistics and literature: Language in the verbal arts of the world*. Oxford: Blackwell.

Feld, Steven. 1982. Sound and sentiment: *Birds, weeping, poetics, and song in Kaluli expression*. 2d ed. Philadelphia: University of Pennsylvania Press.

Finnegan, Ruth. 1992. *Oral traditions and the verbal arts*. London: Routledge.

Fock, Niels. 1963. *Waiwai: Religion and society of an Amazonian tribe*. Copenhagen: National Museum.

Fontanier, Pierre. 1968. *Les figures du discours*. Paris: Flamarion.

Freud, Sigmund. 1905. Jokes and their relation to the unconscious. In *The standard edition of the complete works of Sigmund Freud*, edited by James Strachey and Anna Freud. London: Hogarth [1974].

Friedrich, Paul. 1979. *Language, context, and the imagination*. Stanford, Calif.: Stanford University Press.

———. 1986. *The language parallax: Linguistic relativism and poetic indeterminacy*. Austin: University of Texas Press.

Gal, Susan. 1989. Language and political economy. *Annual Review of Anthropology* 18: 345–367.

Gardner, Martin. 1960. *The annotated Alice*. New York: Meridian.

Garvey, Catherine. 1977. *Play*. Cambridge: Harvard University Press.

Gayton, Ann H., and Stanley S. Newman. 1940. *Yokuts and Western Mono myths*. Anthropological Records, vol. 5, no. 1. Berkeley: University of California Press.

Geertz, Clifford. 1973. *The interpretation of cultures*. New York: Basic Books.

Ginzberg, Louis. 1925. *The legends of the Jews*. Philadelphia: Jewish Publication Society of America.

Goffman, Erving. 1971. *Relations in public: Microstudies of the public order*. New York: Basic Books.

———. 1974. *Frame analysis: An essay on the organization of experience*. New York: Harper and Row.

———. 1976. Replies and responses. *Language in Society* 5: 257–313.

———. 1981. *Forms of talk*. Philadelphia: University of Pennsylvania Press.

———. 1983. The interaction order. *American Sociological Review* 48: 1–17.

Gomez-Peña, Guillermo. 1996. *The new world border: Prophecies, poems, and loqueras for the end of the century*. San Francisco: City Lights.

Gossen, Gary H. 1974. *Chamulas in the world of the sun: Time and space in a Maya oral tradition*. Cambridge: Harvard University Press.

———. 1976. Verbal dueling in Chamula. In *Speech play: Research and resources for studying linguistic creativity*, edited by Barbara Kirshenblatt-Gimblett, 121–146. Philadelphia: University of Pennsylvania Press.

Gradante, William Joseph. 1991. "¡Viva el San Pedro en la Plata!": Tradition, creativity, and folk musical performance in a southern Colombian festival. Ph.D. diss., University of Texas at Austin.

Gupta, Akhil, and James Ferguson, eds. 1997. *Culture power place: Explorations in critical anthropology.* Durham, N.C.: Duke University Press.

Hale, Ken. 1992. Language endangerment and the human value of linguistic diversity. *Language* 68: 35–42.

Hall, Stuart. 1976. *Resistance through rituals: Youth subcultures in postwar Britain.* London: Hutchinson.

Hardesty, Mary. 1977. An ethnography of speaking of the Texas legislature. Master's thesis, University of Texas at Austin.

Haring, Lee. 1992. *Verbal arts in Madagascar: Performance in historical perspective.* Philadelphia: University of Pennsylvania Press.

Heller, Monica, ed. 1988. *Codeswitching: Anthropological and sociolinguistic perspectives.* Berlin: Mouton de Gruyter.

Herndon, Marcia, and McLeod, Norma. 1980. The interrelationship between style and occasion in the Maltese *spirtu pront.* In *The ethnography of musical performance,* edited by Marcia Herndon and Norma McLeod, 147–166. Norwood, Pa.: Norwood Editions.

Hill, Jane. 1985. The grammar of consciousness and the consciousness of grammar. *American Ethnologist* 12: 725–735.

———. 1993. Hasta la vista, baby: Anglo Spanish in the American Southwest. *Critique of Anthropology* 13: 145–176.

Hill, Jane, and Bruce Manheim. 1992. Language and world view. *Annual Review of Anthropology* 21: 381–406.

Hinton, Leanne, Johanna Nichols, and John J. Ohala, eds. 1994. *Sound symbolism.* Cambridge: Cambridge University Press.

Hobart, Mark. 1978. Padi, puns, and the attribution of responsibility. In *Natural symbols in Southeast Asia,* edited by George B. Milner, 55–87. London: School of Oriental and African Studies, University of London.

———. 1990. The patience of plants: A note on agency in Bali. *Rima* 24: 90–135.

Hobsbawm, Eric, and Terrence Ranger, eds. 1983. *The invention of tradition.* Cambridge: Cambridge University Press.

Hockett, Charles F. 1973. Jokes. In *Studies in linguistics: In honor of George L. Trager,* edited by M. Estellie Smith, 153–178. The Hague: Mouton.

Howe, James. 1977. Carrying the village: Kuna political metaphors. In *The social use of metaphor,* edited by J. David Sapir and J. Christopher Crocker, 132–163. Philadelphia: University of Pennsylvania Press.

Howe, James, and Joel Sherzer. 1986. Friend Harryfish and Friend Rattlesnake, or Keeping anthropologists in their place. *Man* 21: 680–696.

Howe, James, Joel Sherzer, and Mac Chapin. 1980. *Cantos y oraciones del congreso Cuna.* Panama City: Editorial Universitaria.

Huizinga, Johan. 1955. *Homo ludens: A study of the play-element in culture.* Boston: Beacon Press.

Hymes, Dell. 1974. *Foundations in sociolinguistics: An ethnographic approach.* Philadelphia: University of Pennsylvania Press.

———. 1981. *"In vain I tried to tell you"*: *Essays in Native American ethnopoetics*. Philadelphia: University of Pennsylvania Press.

———. 1996. *Ethnography, linguistics, narrative inequality: Toward an understanding of voice*. London: Taylor and Francis.

———, ed. 1964. *Language in culture and society: A reader in linguistics and anthropology*. New York: Harper and Row.

Ide, Risako. 1998. Small talk in service encounters: The creation of self and communal space through talk in America. Ph.D. diss., University of Texas at Austin.

Ingham, John. 1984. *Mary, Michael, and Lucifer: Folk catholicism in Central Mexico*. Austin: University of Texas Press.

Jakobson, Roman. 1960. Closing statement: Linguistics and poetry. In *Style in language*, edited by Thomas A. Sebeok, 350–377. Cambridge, Mass.: MIT Press.

———. 1966. Grammatical parallelism and its Russian facet. *Language* 42: 398–429.

———. 1968. Poetry of grammar and grammar of poetry. *Lingua* 21: 597–609.

———. 1971. *Selected writings*. Vol. 2, *Word and language*. The Hague: Mouton.

Jakobson, Roman, and Linda R. Waugh. 1979. *The sound shape of language*. Bloomington: Indiana University Press.

Jameson, Fredric. 1981. *The political unconscious: Narrative as a socially symbolic act*. Ithaca, N.Y.: Cornell University Press.

Janda, Richard D., and Terrell A. Morgan. 1988. El acentó dislocado—pues cantadó—castellanó: On explaining stress-shift in song-texts from Spanish (and certain other Romance languages). In *Advances in Romance linguistics*, edited by David Birdsong and Jean-Pierre Montreuil, 151–170. Dordrecht: Foris.

Jean, Raymond. 2000. *Tutoiements*. Paris: Arléa.

Jefferson, Gail. 1972. Side sequences. In *Studies in social interaction*, edited by David Sudnow, 294–338.

Jenkins, Ron. 1994. *Subversive laughter: The liberating power of comedy*. New York: Free Press.

Johnstone, Barbara, ed. 1994. *Repetition in discourse: Interdisciplinary perspectives*. Norwood, N.J.: Ablex.

Joly, Luz Graciela. 1983. The ritual "play of the Congos" of North Central Panama: Its sociolinguistic implications. Working Papers in Sociolinguistics 85. Austin: Southwest Educational Development Laboratory.

Jones, Leroi, and Larry Neal, eds. 1968. *Black fire: An anthology of Afro-American writing*. New York: Morrow.

Kenney, George. 1998. Caught in Kosovo. *Nation*, July 6, 32.

Kiparsky, Paul. 1973. The role of linguistics in a theory of poetry. In *Language as a human problem*, edited by Einar Haugen and Morton Bloomfield, 233–246. New York: Norton.

Kirshenblatt-Gimblett, Barbara, ed. 1976. *Speech play: Research and resources for studying linguistic creativity*. Philadelphia: University of Pennsylvania Press.

Kluckohn, Clyde, and Dorothea Leighton. 1962. *The Navaho.* Rev. ed. Garden City, N.Y.: Doubleday.

Labov, William. 1972. *Language in the inner city: Studies in the Black English vernacular.* Philadelphia: University of Pennsylvania Press.

Lakoff, George. 1987. *Women, fire, and dangerous things: What categories reveal about the mind.* Chicago: University of Chicago Press.

Lakoff, George, and Mark Johnson. 1980. *Metaphors we live by.* Chicago: University of Chicago Press.

Lausberg, Heinrich. 1960. *Handbuch der literarischen rhetorik.* Munich: Max Hueber Verlag.

Lavenda, Robert H. 1986. Festivals and carnivals. In *Handbook of Latin American popular culture,* edited by Harold E. Hinds Jr. and Charles M. Tatum, 191–205. Westport, Conn.: Greenwood Press.

Le Page, R. B., and Tabouret-Keller, Andrée. 1985. *Acts of identity: Creole-based approaches to language and ethnicity.* Cambridge: Cambridge University Press.

Lee, David. 1992. *Competing discourses: Perspective and ideology in language.* London: Longman.

Legman, Gershon. 1968. *Rationale of the dirty joke: An analysis of sexual humor.* New York: Grove Press.

———, ed. 1974. *The limerick.* New York: Bell.

Léon-Portilla, Miguel. 1969. *Pre-Columbian literatures of Mexico.* Norman: University of Oklahoma Press.

Levin, Samuel R. 1964. Poetry and grammaticalness. In *Proceedings of the Ninth International Congress of Linguists,* edited by Horace G. Lunt, 308–314. The Hague: Mouton.

Levine, Lawrence W. 1977. *Black culture and black consciousness: Afro-American folk thought from slavery to freedom.* Oxford: Oxford University Press.

Limon, José E. 1978. Agringado joking in Texas Mexican society: Folklore and differential identity. In *New directions in Chicano scholarship,* edited by Ricardo Romo and Raymund Paredes, 33–50. La Jolla: Chicano Studies Program, University of California at San Diego.

———. 1982. History, Chicano joking, and the varieties of higher education: Tradition and performance as critical symbolic action. *Journal of the Folklore Institute* 9: 141–166.

Lindenfeld, Jacqueline. 1990. *Speech and sociability at French urban marketplaces.* Amsterdam: John Benjamins.

Lipski, John. 1989. *The speech of the Negros Congos of Panama.* Creole Language Library, vol 4. Philadelphia: John Benjamins.

Mahood, Molly M. 1957. *Shakespeare's wordplay.* London: Methuen.

Mandelbaum, David G., ed. 1963. *Selected writings of Edward Sapir in language, culture, and personality.* Berkeley: University of California Press.

Martínez, Herón Pérez, ed. 1998. *México en fiesta.* Zamora, Michoacán: Colegio de Michoacán.

McCarthy, John J. 1986. OCP effects: Gemination and antigemination. *Linguistic Inquiry* 17: 207–263.

McDowell, John H. 1985. Verbal dueling. In *Handbook of discourse analysis*. Vol. 3, *Discourse and dialogue*, edited by Teun A. Van Dijk, 203–211. London: Academic Press.

Messenger, John C. Jr. 1959. The role of proverbs in a Nigerian judicial system. *Southwestern Journal of Anthropology* 15: 64–73.

Millar, Susanna. 1968. *The psychology of play*. Harmondsworth, England: Penguin Books.

Milne, Jean. 1965. *Fiesta time in Latin America*. Los Angeles: Ward Ritchie Press.

Molière. *L'avare*.

Moravcsik, Edith A. 1992. Reduplication. In *International encyclopedia of linguistics*. Vol. 3, edited by William Bright, 323–324. New York: Oxford University Press.

Nachmanovitch, Stephen. 1990. *Free play: Improvisation in life and art*. Los Angeles: Jeremy P. Tarcher.

Nadel, S. F. 1954. Morality and language among the Nupe. *Man* 64: 55–57.

Nelson, Diane M. 1999. *A finger in the wound: Body politics in quincentennial Guatemala*. Berkeley: University of California Press.

Neruda, Pablo. 1964. *Memorial de isla negra*. Buenos Aires: Editorial Losada.

Newman, Stanley. 1967. Classical Nahuatl. In *Handbook of Middle American Indians*, edited by Norman McQuown, 179–199. Austin: University of Texas Press.

Norrick, Neal R. 1993. *Conversational joking: Humor in everyday talk*. Bloomington: Indiana University Press.

Nuckolls, Janis. 1996. *Sounds like life: Sound-symbolic grammar, performance, and cognition in Paztaza Quechua*. New York: Oxford University Press.

Opie, Iona, and Peter Opie. 1959. *The lore and language of school children*. Oxford: Clarendon Press.

Pagliai, Valentina. 2000. In rhyme I will answer you: Verbal fights and the poetical construction of politics in the Tuscan "Contrasto." In *SALSA VII: Proceedings of the seventh annual Symposium about Language and Society (Austin)*, edited by Nisha Merchant-Goss, Amanda R. Doran, and Anastasia Coles, 153–163. Austin: University of Texas Department of Linguistics.

Palmer, Jerry 1994. *Taking humour seriously*. London: Routledge.

Paredes, Américo. 1977. On ethnographic work among minority groups: A folklorist's perspective. *New Scholar* 6: 1–32.

———. 1991. *Between two worlds*. Houston: Arte Público Press.

Peirce, Charles S. 1932. *Collected papers of C. S. Peirce*, edited by Charles Hartshorne and Paul Weiss. Cambridge: Harvard University Press.

Philips, Susan. 1975. Teasing, punning, and putting people on. Working Papers in Sociolinguistics 28. Austin: Southwest Educational Development Laboratory.

———. 1985. Indian children in Anglo classrooms. In *Language of inequality*, edited by Nessa Wolfson and Joan Manes, 311–323. Berlin: Mouton.

Piaget, Jean. 1951. *Play, dreams, and imitation in childhood*. London: Routledge.

Piddington, Ralph. 1963. *The psychology of laughter: A study in social adaptation*. New York: Gamut Press.

Potter, Russell A. 1995. *Spectacular vernaculars: Hip-hop and the politics of postmodernism*. Albany: State University of New York Press.

Radcliffe-Brown, Alfred R. 1940. On joking relationships. *Africa* 13: 195–210.

Reily, Suzel A. 1998. Brazil: Central and southern areas. In *The Garland encyclopedia of world music*. Vol. 2, *South America, Mexico, Central America, and the Caribbean*, edited by Dale A. Olsen and Daniel E. Shechy, 300–322. New York: Garland.

Rivière, Peter. 1971. The political structure of the Trio Indians as manifested in a system of ceremonial dialogue. In *The translation of culture*, edited by Thomas O. Beidelman, 293–311. London: Tavistock.

Ross, John Robert. 1972. The category squish: Endstation Hauptwort. In *Papers from the eighth regional meeting of the Chicago Linguistic Society*, edited by Paul M. Peranteau, Judith N. Levi, and Gloria C. Phares, 316–328. Chicago: Chicago Linguistic Society.

Rushforth, Scott. 1991. Uses of Bearlake and Mescalero (Athapaskan) classificatory verbs. *International Journal of American Linguistics* 57: 251–266.

Sacks, Harvey. 1973. On some puns: With some intimations. In *Report of the twenty-third annual Roundtable Meeting of Linguistics and Language Studies*, edited by Roger W. Shuy, 135–144. Washington, D.C.: Georgetown University Press.

———. 1974. An analysis of the course of a joke's telling in conversation. In *Explorations in the Ethnography of Speaking*, edited by Richard Bauman and Joel Sherzer, 337–353. Cambridge: Cambridge University Press.

Sammons, Kay, and Joel Sherzer, eds. 2000. *Translating native Latin American verbal art: Ethnopoetics and ethnography of speaking*. Washington, D.C.: Smithsonian Institution Press.

Sanches, Mary, and Barbara Kirshenblatt-Gimblett. 1976. Children's traditional speech play and child language. In *Speech play: Research and resources for studying linguistic creativity*, edited by Mary Sanches and Barbara Kirshenblatt-Gimblett, 65–110. Philadelphia: University of Pennsylvania Press.

Sapir, Edward. 1911. Diminutive and augmentative consonantism in Wishram. In *Handbook of American Indian languages*, edited by Franz Boas, 638–645. Smithsonian Institution, Bureau of American Ethnology Bulletin 40, pt. 1. Washington, D.C.

———. 1915. *Abnormal types of speech in Nootka*. Canada, Department of Mines, Geological Survey, Memoir 62; Anthropological Series, no. 5. Ottawa: Government Printing Bureau.

———. 1921. *Language: An introduction to the study of speech*. New York: Harcourt, Brace and World.

———. 1932. Two Navajo puns. *Language* 8: 217–219.

Schieffelin, Bambi B., Kathryn A. Woolard, and Paul V. Kroskrity, eds. 1998.

Language ideologies: Practice and theory. New York: Oxford University Press.

Schultz, Emily A. 1990. *Dialogue at the margins: Whorf, Bakhtin, and linguistic relativity*. Madison: University of Wisconsin Press.

Scott, James C. 1985. *Weapons of the weak: Everyday forms of peasant resistance*. New Haven: Yale University Press.

———. 1990. *Domination and the arts of resistance: Hidden transcripts*. New Haven: Yale University Press.

Seeger, Anthony. 1986. Oratory is spoken, myth is told, and song is sung, but they are all music to my ears. In *Native South American discourse*, edited by Joel Sherzer and Greg Urban, 59–82. Berlin: Mouton de Gruyter.

Shakespeare, William. *Hamlet*.

———. *Julius Caesar*.

———. *Romeo and Juliet*.

Sherzer, Dina. 1978. Dialogic incongruities in the theater of the absurd. *Semiotica* 22: 269–285.

Sherzer, Dina, and Joel Sherzer. 1976. *Mormaknamaloe*: The Cuna mola. In *Ritual and symbol in Native Central America*, edited by Philip Young and James Howe, 21–42. University of Oregon Anthropological Papers 9. Eugene: University of Oregon.

———, eds. 1987. *Humor and comedy in puppetry: Celebration in popular culture*. Bowling Green, Ohio: Bowling Green State University Popular Press.

Sherzer, Joel. 1978a. Cuna numeral classifiers. In *Linguistic and literary studies in honor of Archibald A. Hill*, edited by Mohammad A. Jazayery, Edgar C. Polomé, and Werner Winter, 331–337. The Hague: Mouton.

———. 1978b. Oh! That's a pun and I didn't mean it. *Semiotica* 22: 335–350.

———. 1982. Play languages: With a note on ritual languages. In *Exceptional language and linguistics*, edited by Loraine K. Obler and Lisa Menn, 175–199. New York: Academic Press.

———. 1983. *Kuna ways of speaking: An ethnographic perspective*. Austin: University of Texas Press.

———. 1987. A discourse-centered approach to language and culture. *American Anthropologist* 89: 295–309.

———. 1988. Talk about *tu* and *vous*. In *Languages and cultures: Studies in honor of Edgar C. Polomé*, edited by Mohammad A. Jazayery and Werner Winter, 611–620. Berlin: Mouton de Gruyter.

———. 1989. The Kuna verb: A study in the interplay of grammar, discourse, and style. In *General and Amerindian ethnolinguistics: In remembrance of Stanley Newman*, edited by Mary R. Key and Henry Hoenigswald, 261–272. Berlin: Mouton de Gruyter.

———. 1990. *Verbal art in San Blas: Kuna culture through its discourse*. Cambridge: Cambridge University Press.

———. 1992. Modes of representation and translation of Native American discourse. Examples from the San Blas Kuna. In *On the translation of Na-*

tive American literatures, edited by Brian Swann, 426–440. Washington, D.C.: Smithsonian Institution Press.

———. 1993. On puns, comebacks, verbal dueling, and play languages: Speech play in Balinese verbal life. *Language in Society* 22: 217–233.

———. 1994. The Kuna and Columbus: Encounters and confrontations of discourse. *American Anthropologist* 96: 1–23.

———. 1997. Turtle and Jaguar: A Kuna animal story in cultural context. *Latin American Indian Literatures Journal* 12: 1–16.

Sherzer, Joel, and Greg Urban, eds. 1986. *Native South American discourse.* Berlin: Mouton.

Sherzer, Joel, and Anthony Woodbury, eds. 1987. *Native American discourse: Poetics and rhetoric.* Cambridge: Cambridge University Press.

Slater, Candace. 1982. *Stories on a string: The Brazilian literatura de cordel.* Berkeley: University of California Press.

Smith, Ronald R. 1998. Panama. In *The Garland encyclopedia of world music.* Vol. 2, *South America, Mexico, Central America, and the Caribbean,* edited by Dale A. Olsen and Daniel E. Shechy, 770–785. New York: Garland.

Smith, William George. 1948. *The Oxford dictionary of English proverbs.* 2d rev. ed. Oxford: Clarendon.

Smitherman, Geneva. 1977. *Talkin and testifyin: The language of Black America.* Boston: Houghton Mifflin.

———. 1994. *Black talk: Words and phrases from the hood to the amen corner.* Boston: Houghton Mifflin.

Solomon, Thomas. 1994. Coplas de Todos Santos in Cochabamba: Language, music, and performance in Bolivian Quechua song dueling. *Journal of American Folklore* 107: 378–414.

Stratton, Richard, and Kim Wozencraft, eds. 1998. *Slam.* New York: Grove Press.

Tedlock, Dennis. 1983. *The spoken word and the work of interpretation.* Philadelphia: University of Pennsylvania Press.

———, trans. 1985. *Popol Vuh: The definitive edition of the Mayan book of the dawn of life and the glories of gods and kings.* New York: Simon and Schuster.

Thomas, Dylan. 1971. *The poems of Dylan Thomas.* New York: New Directions.

Thorne, James Peter. 1965. Stylistics and generative grammars. *Journal of Linguistics* 1: 49–59.

Thun, Nils. 1963. *Reduplicative words in English: A study of formations of the types tick-tock, hurly burly, and shilly-shally.* Uppsala: Carl Bloms Boktryckeri A.-B.

Traugott, Elizabeth Closs, and Mary Louise Pratt. 1980. *Linguistics for students of literature.* New York: Harcourt Brace Jovanovich.

Vickers, Adrian. 1989. *Bali: A paradise created.* Berkeley: Periplus Editions.

Wallis, Richard H. 1980. The voice as a mode of cultural expression in Bali. Ph.D. diss., University of Michigan.

Weeda, Donald Stanton. 1992. Word truncation in prosodic morphology. Ph.D. diss., University of Texas at Austin.

Weinreich, Max. 1980. *History of the Yiddish language*. Chicago: University of Chicago Press.

Wells, Carolyn. 1963. *A whimsey anthology*. New York: Dover.

Whorf, Benjamin Lee. 1956. *Language, thought, and reality: Selected writings of Benjamin Lee Whorf*. Cambridge: MIT Press.

Wilson, Christopher P. 1979. *Jokes: Form, content, use, and function*. London: Academic Press.

Withers, Carl. 1948. *A rocket in my pocket: The rhymes and chants of young Americans*. New York: Holt, Rinehart and Winston.

Wyman, Leland C. 1970. *Blessingway*. Tucson: University of Arizona Press.

Yaguello, Marina. 1998. *Language through the looking glass: Exploring language and linguistics*. Oxford: Oxford University Press.

Yankah, Kwesi. 1986. Proverb rhetoric and African judicial processes: The untold story. *Journal of American Folklore* 99: 280–303.

Yip, Moira. 1982. Reduplication and C-V skeleta in Chinese secret languages. *Linguistic Inquiry* 13: 637–661.

Zepeda, Ofelia. 1995. *Ocean power: Poems from the desert*. Tucson: University of Arizona Press.

Zurbuchen, Mary S. 1987. *The language of Balinese shadow theater*. Princeton: Princeton University Press.

Credits

Acknowledgment is hereby made to the owners of the following copyrighted material:

Chapter 3

My discussion of puns draws on Sherzer 1978b. Reprinted by permission of Mouton de Gruyter.

My discussion of Balinese speech play draws on Sherzer 1993. Reprinted by permission of Cambridge University Press.

Colombian coplas are reprinted from Gradante 1991. Reprinted by permission of William Gradante.

Chapter 4

Colombian coplas are reprinted from Gradante 1991. Reprinted by permission of William Gradante.

Selections from performances/texts of the Kuna Indians of Panama are from Sherzer 1990. Reprinted by permission of Cambridge University Press.

"Wordsworth" is from Bombaugh 1961: 43. Reprinted by permission of Dover Publications.

The wine glass is from Wells 1963: 17. Reprinted by permission of Dover Publications.

"Jabberwocky" is from Lewis 1951: 133. Reprinted by permission of Simon and Schuster Books for Young Readers, an imprint of Simon and Schuster Children's Publishing Division.

"A Process in the Weather of the Heart," by Dylan Thomas, is from *The Poems of Dylan Thomas*, copyright © 1939 by New Directions Publishing Corp. Reprinted by permission of New Directions Publishing Corp.

"Cloud Song from Ocean Power," by Ofelia Zepeda, copyright © 1995 by Ofelia Zepeda. Reprinted by permission of the University of Arizona Press and the author.

"The Mexico-Texan," by Américo Paredes, is reprinted, by permission of the publisher, from *Between Two Worlds* (Houston: Arte Público Press, 1991).

"When raza?" by Alurista, is from Alurista 1971: 1. Reprinted by permission of the University of California, Los Angeles, Chicano Studies Research Center.

Selections from Anzaldúa 1987: 77, 81–82, are reprinted by permission of the publisher, Aunt Lute Books.

Selection from "Bludoo Baby, Want Money, and Alligator Got It to Give," by Amiri Baraka, is from Jones and Neal 1968: 299. Reprinted by permission of Sterling Lord Literistic, Inc.

Selections from "To all sisters," by Saul Williams, and "The sweetest revolutionary," by Jessica Care Moore, are from Stratton and Wozencraft 1998: 52, 299. Reprinted by permission of Grove/Atlantic, Inc.

The Suya curing song is from Seeger 1986. Reprinted by permission of Mouton de Gruyter.

A portion of "The Way of Basil" is from Sherzer 1992. Reprinted by permission of Smithsonian Institution Press.

EVERY EFFORT has been made to locate the copyright owners and seek permission to use their copyrighted material appearing in this publication. In those instances where attempts were unsuccessful but the copyright owner becomes aware of my use of their material, I welcome their contacting the publisher.

Index

CPSIA information can be obtained
at www.ICGtesting.com
Printed in the USA
JSHW030206140722
28037JS00001B/119